IT Control Objectives for Sarbanes-Oxley

4th Edition | Using COBIT 2019

COBIT®
An ISACA® Framework

ISACA®

About ISACA

For more than 50 years, ISACA® (*www.isaca.org*) has advanced the best talent, expertise and learning in technology. ISACA equips individuals with knowledge, credentials, education and community to progress their careers and transform their organizations, and enables enterprises to train and build quality teams that effectively drive IT audit, risk management and security priorities forward. ISACA is a global professional association and learning organization that leverages the expertise of more than 150,000 members who work in information security, governance, assurance, risk and privacy to drive innovation through technology. It has a presence in 188 countries, including more than 220 chapters worldwide. In 2020, ISACA launched One In Tech, a philanthropic foundation that supports IT education and career pathways for under-resourced, under-represented populations.

Disclaimer

ISACA has designed and created *IT Control Objectives for Sarbanes-Oxley, 4th Edition, Using COBIT 2019* (the "Work") primarily as an educational resource for professionals. ISACA makes no claim that use of any of the Work will assure a successful outcome. The Work should not be considered inclusive of all proper information, procedures and tests or exclusive of other information, procedures and tests that are reasonably directed to obtaining the same results. In determining the propriety of any specific information, procedure or test, professionals should apply their own professional judgment to the specific circumstances presented by the particular systems or information technology environment.

ISACA
1700 E. Golf Road, Suite 400
Schaumburg, IL 60173, USA
Phone: +1.847.660.5505
Fax: +1.847.253.1755
Contact us: https://support.isaca.org
Website: www.isaca.org

Participate in the ISACA Online Forums: https://engage.isaca.org/onlineforums

Twitter: http://twitter.com/ISACANews
LinkedIn: www.linkedin.com/company/isaca
Facebook: www.facebook.com/ISACAGlobal
Instagram: www.instagram.com/isacanews/

IT Control Objectives for Sarbanes-Oxley, 4th Edition, Using COBIT 2019
ISBN 978-1-60420-892-4

Acknowledgments

ISACA would like to recognize:

Lead Developers

Francine McKenna, CPA (Registered), American University and The Digging Company LLC, USA
Dina Numan, CRISC, CDPSE, COBIT Assessor, ITIL, ScanWave C.T.S., Jordan

Expert Reviewers

Anagha Apte, CISA, CISM, CGEIT, CRISC, Birlasoft Solutions, Inc., USA
Hans Henrik Aabenhus Berthing, CISA, CISM, CGEIT, CRISC, CIA, CL, State Authorized Public Accountant, Denmark
Sarat Chegu, CISA, CGEIT, CRISC, FCA, Isafe Consulting, India
Deepinder Chhabra, CISA, CISM, CGEIT, CRISC, CDPSE, CCISO, CISSP, Verizon, UK
Joyce Chua, CISA, CISM, CDPSE, CCISO, CFE, CIA, CIPP(A), CIPP(E), CIPM, FIP, IRCA, ISMS Associate Auditor, ITIL, MCP, PMP, UOB Group, Singapore
Shigeto Fukuda, CISA, CDPSE, EYSCC, Japan
Ashish Gupta, CISA, CRISC, CDPSE, Ernst & Young, Netherlands
J. Winston Hayden, CISA, CISM, CGEIT, CRISC, CDPSE, South Africa
Gary David Langham, CISA, CISM, CGEIT, CISSP, CPFA, Australia
Michael Malcolm, CISA, CIA, CISSP, CRMA, OpenText Corporation, Canada
Raphael Otieno Onyango, CISA, COBIT 5 Foundation, CIDA, CPA, ECLOF, Kenya
Andre Pitkowski, CGEIT, CRISC, Professor, Centro Universitário Senac São Paulo, Brazil
Sreechith Radhakrishnan, CISA, CISM, CGEIT, CRISC, CDPSE, COBIT 5 Assessor, ISO 20000 Master, ITIL Expert, Lean Six Sigma Black Belt, PMP, Global Success Systems FZ, LLC, UAE
Abdul Rafeq, CISA, FCA Wincer InfoTech Ltd., India
Salomon Rico, CISA, CISM, CGEIT, Deloitte Spanish Latin America, Mexico

Board of Directors

Gregory Touhill, Chair, CISM, CISSP, Director, CERT Center, Carnegie Mellon University, USA
Pamela Nigro, Vice-Chair, CISA, CGEIT, CRISC, CDPSE, CRMA, Vice President–Information Technology, Security Officer, Home Access Health, USA
John De Santis, Former Chairman and Chief Executive Officer, HyTrust, Inc., USA
Niel Harper, CISA, CRISC, CDPSE, Chief Information Security Officer, UNOPS, Denmark
Gabriela Hernandez-Cardoso, Independent Board Member, Mexico
Maureen O'Connell, Board Chair, Acacia Research (NASDAQ), Former Chief Financial Officer and Chief Administration Officer, Scholastic, Inc., USA
David Samuelson, Chief Executive Officer, ISACA, USA
Gerrard Schmid, President and Chief Executive Officer, Diebold Nixdorf, USA
Veronica Rose, CISA, CDPSE, Founder, Encrypt Africa, Kenya
Asaf Weisberg, CISA, CRISC, CISM, CGEIT, Chief Executive Officer, introSight Ltd., Israel
Tracey Dedrick, ISACA Board Chair, 2020-2021, Former Chief Risk Officer, Hudson City Bancorp, USA
Brennan P. Baybeck, CISA, CRISC, CISM, CISSP, ISACA Board Chair, 2019-2020, Vice President and Chief Information Security Officer for Customer Services, Oracle Corporation, USA
Rob Clyde, CISM, ISACA Board Chair, 2018-2019, Independent Director, Titus, and Executive Chair, White Cloud Security, USA

Page intentionally left blank

TABLE OF CONTENTS

LIST OF FIGURES

Chapter 1. Introduction and Purpose

Chapter 2. Requirements of PCAOB Auditing Standard 2201

Chapter 3. Role of the COSO Framework and Its Relationship to COBIT 2019

Chapter 4. Application Controls

Chapter 6. IT Sarbanes-Oxley Compliance Road Map

Appendix A. Entity-Level/Activity-Level and IT General Controls for Sarbanes-Oxley

Appendix B. COBIT 2019 Governance and Management Objectives Mapped to COSO Components and Principles

Appendix C. Example Application Controls

Appendix D. Example Application and Technology Inventory

Appendix E. Example SOX ITGC Control Matrix

Appendix F. Example Sarbanes-Oxley Control Narrative

Appendix G. Example Remediation Log

Chapter 1
Introduction and Purpose

1.1 Introduction

IT Control Objectives for Sarbanes-Oxley, 4th Edition, Using COBIT 2019 provides guidance on the assessment of effectiveness of internal control over financial reporting (ICFR) by internal auditors, in attestation of the management assessment, to comply with the Sarbanes-Oxley Act of 2002 (SOX). This guide is not for the assessment of enterprise governance of information and technology (EGIT).

This fourth edition of the guide incorporates updated guidance and standards from the Public Company Accounting Oversight Board (PCAOB) and the American Institute of Certified Public Accountants (AICPA®) and its Auditing Standards Board (ASB), and the renaming and renumbering of PCAOB standards related to ICFR, e.g., the renaming and reorganizing of Auditing Standard 5 (AS 5) to Auditing Standard 2201 (AS 2201) and guidance related to audits provided by service organizations. This edition provides guidance for implementing ICFR using COBIT® 2019, for IT and financial management within enterprises and for their internal and external auditors and consultants.

In 2018, ISACA released COBIT 2019, an updated version of the COBIT® framework that incorporates several enhancements. Many enterprises that are subject to the Sarbanes-Oxley Act use COBIT as a foundation for their systems of governance and internal control in a technology environment. This fourth edition incorporates the COBIT 2019 framework and its governance and management objectives and aligns with *COBIT® Focus Area: Information and Technology Risk*.

The Committee of Sponsoring Organizations' (COSO) Internal Control – Integrated Framework is used by many enterprises to meet their responsibilities under the Sarbanes-Oxley Act to maintain a system of ICFR. Because ISACA closely aligns the COBIT frameworks to the COSO framework, it is important to show how the COSO framework aligns with COBIT 2019. This edition provides the mapping of the role of COSO Internal Control – Integrated Framework 2013 to COBIT 2019. The COSO and COBIT 2019 frameworks are complementary and compatible guidance to support the assessment and improvement of internal control practices and activities within enterprise governance and management.

Rapid digital transformation makes information and technology (I&T) crucial to the support, sustainability and growth of enterprises. This fourth edition of *IT Control Objectives for Sarbanes-Oxley* includes a new chapter[1] that highlights technological innovations, e.g., big data, cloud computing, virtual supply chains, artificial intelligence (AI) and a universal dependence on connectivity, and their profound impacts on auditing IT controls in an increasingly virtual world. I&T change is occurring faster than expected—especially after the significant impact of the COVID-19 pandemic on how enterprises and auditors (internal and external) ensure the timeliness, accuracy and integrity of financial statements remotely using technology.

This SOX guidance supports the SOX requirement to comply with various personally identifiable information (PII) protection acts, especially as they relate to theft, fraud and security of PII.

1.2 Target Audience

The primary audience of this guide includes the following:

- Internal auditors
- External auditors

[1] See Chapter 7, New Technology Affecting ICFR. This chapter leverages ISACA's *COBIT® 2019 Design Guide: Designing an Information and Technology Governance Solution*, USA, 2018, *https://store.isaca.org/s/store#/store/browse/detail/a2S4w000004Ko9bEAC*, and its companion tool kit, which may be downloaded at *https://www.isaca.org/-/media/files/isacadp/project/isaca/knowledge-and-insights/zips/cobit-2019-design-toolkit_tkt_eng_1218.zip?la=en&hash=0E8BC92071EF5FDF474A979F75A0F78CBC775E54*.

- IT auditors
- IT managers
- Financial and operational managers

1.3 Need for IT Control Guidance

Financial reporting processes remain extremely reliant on IT systems. Such systems, whether enterprise resource planning (ERP), cloud-based or other, e.g., SAP®, Oracle NetSuite®, Microsoft Dynamics 365® or Workday®, are deeply integrated in initiating, authorizing, recording, processing and reporting financial transactions. Therefore, IT systems are inextricably linked to the overall financial reporting process and need to be assessed, along with other important processes, for compliance with the ICFR provisions of the Sarbanes-Oxley Act.

1.4 PCAOB Auditing Standards and Management Assessment of ICFR

SOX established the Public Company Accounting Oversight Board (PCAOB). PCAOB's mission is to protect the interests of investors and further the public interest in the preparation of informative, accurate and independent audit reports. The PCAOB is an independent, not-for-profit regulator of the auditors of enterprises subject to US securities laws, replacing audit industry self-regulation by the AICPA. The Securities and Exchange Commission (SEC) provides oversight of the PCAOB budget and activities, such as inspections of audit firms, establishment of auditing standards, and enforcement and disciplinary activities related to audit firm and audit firm individual violation of those standards.

The PCAOB is required under SOX to register and regulate the auditors of issuers who are SEC registrants and to establish and monitor compliance with auditing standards for the audit of SEC registrants. In 2003, the PCAOB published AS 2, the auditing standard that provided the initial requirements for audits of the effectiveness of ICFR according to the new Sarbanes-Oxley law. In 2007, AS 5 superseded AS 2, with a goal of simplifying requirements for ICFR audits via a top-down, risk-based approach to the design and execution of the audits of ICFR.

In March 2015, the PCAOB announced the adoption of amendments to reorganize its auditing standards using a topical structure and a single, integrated numbering system. As a result of this initiative, AS 2201: *An Audit of Internal Control Over Financial Reporting That Is Integrated with An Audit of Financial Statements* superseded AS 5. Additional standards found in the "Special Topics" section on the PCAOB site are of specific interest to internal auditors. Examples are AS 2601: *Consideration of an Entity's Use of a Service Organization* and AS 2605: *Consideration of the Internal Audit Function.*[2]

1.5 Internal Control Definition

Internal control is a process designed by, or under the supervision of, the registrant's principal executive and principal financial officers, or persons performing similar functions, and effected by the registrant's board of directors, management and other personnel to provide reasonable assurance regarding the reliability of financial reporting and the preparation of financial statements for external purposes in accordance with generally accepted accounting principals.

[2] AS 1005: *Independence*, AS 1010: *Training and Proficiency of the Independent Auditor* and AS 1015: *Due Professional Care in the Performance of Work* are also applicable to an audit of internal control over financial reporting.

The COSO 2013 Internal Control – Integrated Framework defines internal control as follows:

> *Internal control is a process, effected by an entity's board of directors, management, and other personnel, designed to provide reasonable assurance regarding the achievement of objectives relating to operations, reporting, and compliance.*[3]

This definition of internal control is broad. The provisions of the Sarbanes-Oxley Act relate explicitly to the effectiveness of ICFR and not to all the elements of internal control that the COSO framework describes. The SEC defines controls in the context of ICFR as:

> *...a specific set of policies, procedures, and activities designed to meet an objective. A control may exist within a designated function or activity in a process. A control's impact...may be entity-wide or specific to an account balance, class of transactions or application. Controls have unique characteristics—for example, they can be: automated or manual; reconciliations; segregation of duties (SoD); review and approval authorizations; safeguarding and accountability of assets; preventing or detecting error or fraud. Controls within a process may consist of financial reporting controls and operational controls (that is, those designed to achieve operational objectives).*[4]

1.6 SOX Relationship With Other Regulatory Compliance and Private Enterprises

Many enterprises that must comply with the requirements of the Sarbanes-Oxley Act to maintain a system of ICFR are also subject to other regulatory compliance requirements. For example, health care providers may need to comply with the Health Insurance Portability and Accountability Act (HIPAA), and financial institutions are concerned about compliance with BASEL III and the Gramm-Leach-Bliley Act (GLBA). In addition, the Payment Card Industry Data Security Standard (PCI DSS), California Consumer Privacy Act (CCPA) and the European Union (EU) General Data Protection Regulation (GDPR) have impact for enterprises across industries. Enterprises often leverage their SOX internal control compliance as a foundation for these other compliance requirements.

The level of detail of other regulatory compliance regimes may vary compared to the SOX ICFR requirements. Some regulations are more prescriptive, such as PCI DSS. Others may have similar requirements, but different parameters, such as data retention periods. Yet, enterprise identification, implementation and maintenance of internal controls has a high degree of alignment with the implementation of many other regulatory frameworks, regardless of the source or reason for the requirements. Maintaining compliance with SOX ICFR requirements supports the ultimate objective of meeting all other compliance requirements.

The Sarbanes-Oxley Act officially applies only to publicly traded companies in the United States and wholly owned subsidiaries and foreign companies that are publicly traded and do business in the United States. However, many other enterprises around the world are subject to similar or identical compliance regimes in their industry or country. For example, in the United States, larger insurance enterprises are subject to ICFR, whether or not their securities are publicly traded on securities exchanges. Other enterprises, such as not-for-profit organizations and governmental agencies, adopt the standard voluntarily or by specific national requirements. Yet others, such as large private enterprises, are encouraged to apply the standard by their finance providers. Therefore, many other enterprises in addition to publicly traded enterprises are maintaining systems of internal controls over financial reporting or are subject to audit on these controls for the Sarbanes-Oxley Act.

Beyond the compliance requirements for SEC registrants, several reporting environments are strongly influenced by SOX. For example, J-SOX is the unofficial term for the Japan Financial Instruments and Exchange Act that was finalized in 2007 to ensure that corporate information is disclosed in a fair manner to investors.[5] In India, clause 49

[3] COSO, "Internal Control – Integrated Framework, Executive Summary," May 2013, *www.coso.org/Documents/990025P-Executive-Summary-final-may20.pdf.* Used with permission.
[4] US Securities and Exchange Commission, "Commission Guidance Regarding Management's Report on Internal Control Over Financial Reporting Under Section 13(a) or 15(d) of the Securities Exchange Act of 1934," 17 CFR Part 241, 2007, *www.sec.gov/rules/interp/2007/33-8810.pdf*
[5] EisnerAmper, "J-SOX Versus U.S. Sarbanes Oxley Act Specifics of J-SOX Requirements," 2017, *www.eisneramper.com/j-sox-sarbanes-oxley-act/*

of the stock exchange listing requirements for public companies is similar to SOX.[6] The Directive 2006/43/EC of the European Parliament and of the Council of 17 May 2006, which became EU law in 2009, imposes requirements on audit committees that have strong similarities to the ICFR provisions of SOX.[7] These regulatory changes, and several others around the world, signal that the impact of SOX is well beyond the regulation of SEC registrants in the United States.

1.7 How to Use This Publication

The information contained in this publication provides useful guidance and tools for enterprises that are trying to prepare and sustain their IT organizations relative to SOX compliance. However, each enterprise should carefully consider the appropriate IT control objectives (COBIT 2019 governance and management practices) that are necessary for its own circumstances.

Enterprises may choose not to include all the control objectives discussed in this guide. Similarly, they may choose to include control objectives not discussed in this guide. In either case, it is expected that each organization will customize descriptions of control objectives and examples to reflect the specific circumstances of the enterprise.

This guide was developed in a modular fashion, which allows readers to go to specific topics and appendices as opposed to reading the guide from cover to cover. For example, many experienced SOX and COBIT users have used the previous edition of *IT Control Objectives for Sarbanes-Oxley* to develop their IT general control templates. These users can update those templates with the revised COBIT 2019 content. They may want to refer to Appendix A, which contains all the revised COBIT 2019 content about entity and IT general controls.

Chapter 3 shows how the guidance in the COSO framework relates to COBIT 2019 for purposes of Sarbanes-Oxley compliance. Appendix B gives a more detailed mapping of COBIT 2019 to the 2013 COSO Internal Control – Integrated Framework, at a control-objective level for Sarbanes-Oxley selected processes.

Chapter 4, about application controls, can be used in conjunction with Appendix C, which gives examples of application controls. The chapter includes a new discussion of automated testing of application controls and application controls in a cloud environment. Readers who want to learn more about the PCAOB changes and, specifically, the new standard AS 2201, should focus on Chapter 2.

Chapter 5 should be used by readers who require information about the role of third-party service organizations and their reports for ICFR.

Chapter 6 should be used by readers who want to refresh their knowledge of how internal controls are maintained and how internal and external auditors audit the effectiveness of those internal controls under COBIT 2019.

Chapter 7 should be used by readers who want to become more familiar with new technologies that are introducing challenges for auditors assessing ICFR, especially IT general controls and controls over security and privacy. The chapter is not exhaustive but, instead, suggests guides and other resources for further information.

1.7.1 Terminology

To be consistent with the language of internal controls and control objectives that are required for Sarbanes-Oxley, this publication uses the language of internal controls and control objectives as defined by COSO. In the transition from COBIT 5 to COBIT 2019, the same terminology, "governance and management practices," is used. In this publication, the terms of governance and management practices and activities in COBIT 2019 are converted to the terms of control objectives and control activities in the Sarbanes-Oxley environment.

[6] Securities and Exchange Board of India, "Corporate Governance in listed Companies - Clause 49 of the Listing Agreement," 26 August 2003, *https://www.sebi.gov.in/legal/circulars/aug-2003/corporate-governance-in-listed-companies-clause-49-of-the-listing-agreement_15948.html*

[7] European Parliament, Council of the European Union, DIRECTIVE 2006/43/EC OF THE EUROPEAN PARLIAMENT AND OF THE COUNCIL of 17 May 2006 on statutory audits of annual accounts and consolidated accounts, amending Council Directives 78/660/EEC and 83/349/EEC and repealing Council Directive 84/253/EEC, *https://eur-lex.europa.eu/legal-content/EN/TXT/PDF/?uri=CELEX:32006L0043&rid=3*

This language conversion is critical to demonstrate how COBIT 2019 can be used to enhance the effectiveness of internal controls over financial reporting. This publication was developed with a very granular use of specific objectives in COBIT 2019 for the requirements of Sarbanes-Oxley compliance. The intention of this guide is not to demonstrate how to achieve broad assurance on EGIT.

1.7.2 Related Publications

The following ISACA publications are particularly important as a foundation for this updated guide:

- *COBIT® 2019 Framework: Governance and Management Objectives*[8]
- *COBIT Focus Area: Information and Technology Risk Using COBIT 2019*[9]

1.7.3 Edition History

Earlier editions of *IT Control Objectives for Sarbanes-Oxley* provided the following updated information:

- The second edition, published in 2006, incorporated the COBIT 4.0 IT governance framework and a top-down risk-based approach based on lessons learned from the implementation of the PCAOB Auditing Standard No. 2.
- The third edition, published in 2014, provided new and revised guidance and standards from ISACA, the PCAOB and the AICPA ASB regarding the change from AS 2 to AS 5. Further, the third edition incorporated a revised edition of the COSO Internal Control – Integrated Framework—the framework adopted by most SEC registrants.

1.8 Using COBIT 2019 Components of the Governance System

COBIT 2019 enables I&T to be governed and managed in a holistic manner for the entire enterprise, while considering the end-to-end business and IT functional areas of responsibility. COBIT 2019 also makes a clear distinction between governance and management. COBIT 2019 organizes 40 governance and management objectives that are grouped into five domains (**figure 1.1**). The domain names are verbs that express the key purpose and areas of activity of the objectives contained in them:

- Evaluate, Direct and Monitor (EDM)
- Align, Plan and Organize (APO)
- Build, Acquire and Implement (BAI)
- Deliver, Service and Support (DSS)
- Monitor, Evaluate and Assess (MEA)

[8] ISACA, *COBIT® 2019 Framework: Governance and Management Objectives*, USA, 2018, *https://store.isaca.org/s/store#/store/browse/detail/a2S4w000004Ko5aEAC*
[9] ISACA, *COBIT Focus Area: Information and Technology Risk*, USA, 2021, *https://store.isaca.org/s/store#/store/browse/detail/a2S4w000004KmAREA0*

Figure 1.1—COBIT Core Model

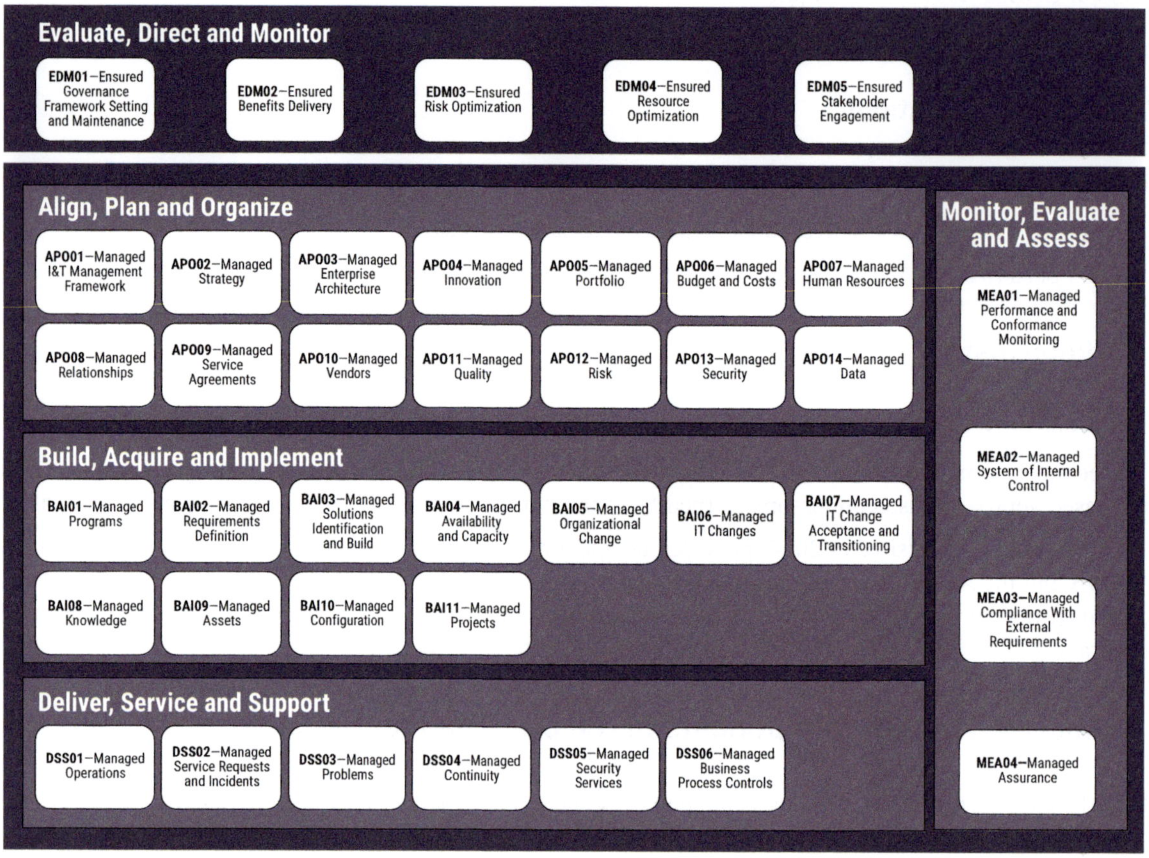

Source: ISACA, *COBIT® 2019 Framework: Introduction and Methodology*, USA, 2018, figure 4.2
https://store.isaca.org/s/store#/store/browse/detail/a2S4w000004Ko5dEAC

The COBIT 2019 framework introduces the term components, which were called enablers in COBIT 5.

- Components are factors that, individually and collectively, contribute to the good operations of the enterprise governance system over I&T.
- Components interact with each other, resulting in a holistic governance system for I&T.
- Components can be of different types. The most familiar are processes. However, components of a governance system also include organizational structures; principles, policies and procedures; information; culture, ethics and behavior; people, skills and competencies; and services, infrastructure and applications (**figure 1.2**).

Figure 1.2—COBIT Components of a Governance System

Source: ISACA, *COBIT® 2019 Framework: Introduction and Methodology*, USA, 2018, figure 4.3, *https://store.isaca.org/s/store#/store/browse/detail/a2S4w000004Ko5dEAC*

Processes are a key component for SOX compliance. *COBIT® 2019 Framework: Governance and Management Objectives* is the source for information about COBIT 2019 processes. The alignment of COBIT 2019 objectives to PCAOB AS 2201 in Chapter 2 and the detailed guidance of entity and general IT controls in Appendix A are linked.

The other COBIT 2019 governance system components are also important to SOX compliance, because they function through processes and for purposes of SOX compliance control objectives and control activities:

- The principles, policies and frameworks component includes the organizational principles and policies, which are key internal controls that are defined by PCAOB AS 2201: *An Audit of Internal Control Over Financial Reporting That Is Integrated with An Audit of Financial Statements* and COSO. Principles and policies are included in entity and general IT controls in most of the 40 governance and management objectives that are outlined in COBIT 2019. Examples of entity and general IT controls are outlined in detail in Appendix A. An organizational principles and policies framework is the vehicle by which governance decisions are institutionalized within the enterprise. Principles and policies are an interaction between governance decisions (direction setting) and management (execution of the decisions).
- Organizational structures are the key decision-making entities in an enterprise. Many good practices for organizational structures specify to have a formal operating principle, defined composition, established span of control, defined levels of authority, delegation of authority and escalation procedures to handle any problems in making decisions. For example, the entity-level COBIT 2019 objectives EDM01 *Ensured Governance Framework Setting and Maintenance* and APO01 *Managed I&T Management Framework* include controls that are related to organizational structures at the governance and management level, respectively. Readers of this guide are encouraged to use the responsible, accountable, consulted and informed (RACI) charts that are

outlined in *COBIT® 2019 Framework: Governance and Management Objectives* to aid in the development of structures and reporting lines.

- The culture, ethics and behavior component addresses enterprise ethics (i.e., tone at the top) and individual ethics and behaviors, which include risk taking, following policy and addressing negative outcomes. This component is one of the key entity-level controls and a key part of the COSO Controls Environment. For Sarbanes-Oxley purposes, COBIT 2019 objectives EDM01 *Ensured Governance Framework Setting and Maintenance* and APO01 *Managed I&T Management Framework* include activities to embed enterprise integrity and ethical value aspects within the governance and management framework. COBIT 2019 objective APO07 *Managed Human Resources* includes activities to address integrity and ethical value aspects from a human resources perspective.
- The information component addresses a key resource for all enterprises. From the time that information is created to the moment it is destroyed, technology plays a significant role. The COBIT 2019 information item component model describes three main quality criteria for information and 15 sub criteria. These criteria are divided into intrinsic, contextual and security/privacy/accessibility categories. Considering each of these quality criteria helps enterprises verify the information that supports enterprise business goals and related control objectives. Information can be considered one stage in the information cycle of an enterprise. In the information cycle, business processes generate and process data, transforming data into information and knowledge. Information adds to the knowledge of people working within the enterprise, which eventually assists them in creating value within the enterprise.
- Services, infrastructure and applications are key resources that are leveraged in the delivery of I&T-related services. These resources are featured heavily in the activity-level general IT controls that are used in this publication to meet Sarbanes-Oxley requirements. Services can be delivered by internal or external parties. Each service capability has a life cycle. A typical life cycle includes the phases of plan, design, build/acquire, use/operate, evaluate/monitor and update/dispose. Various activity-level general IT controls ensure that enterprise goals are ultimately met through the service capabilities that are deployed within the enterprise.
- The people, skills and competencies component addresses skills and competencies for the people (internal and external) who work for the enterprise. Skills need to be developed (e.g., through training) or acquired (e.g., through recruitment) and deployed in various roles within the organizational structure. Skills may need to be redeployed (e.g., if an activity is automated or outsourced).

An enterprise must know its current skill base and plan for the level at which it needs to be. This planning is influenced by the strategy and goals of the enterprise (among other issues). Periodically (e.g., on an annual basis), the enterprise needs to assess the skill base to understand the evolution that has occurred. The assessment results feed into the planning process for the next period. The assessment can also feed into the reward and recognition process for human resources.

Chapter 2
Requirements of PCAOB Auditing Standard 2201

2.1 Introduction

This chapter summarizes the requirements of PCAOB AS 2201, which addresses the requirements of Sections 302 and 404 of the Sarbanes-Oxley Act of 2002. The chapter also discusses additional standards that provide guidance on the internal auditor's role in the external auditors' attestation of ICFR and reliance on the work of third-party service organizations.

PCAOB AS 2201*: An Audit of Internal Control Over Financial Reporting That Is Integrated with An Audit of Financial Statements* has superseded AS 5: *An Audit of Internal Control Over Financial Reporting That Is Integrated with An Audit of Financial Statements* since March 2015. AS 2201 establishes the requirements and provides direction for external auditors who perform an audit of the management assessment of the effectiveness of ICFR that is integrated with an audit of the financial statements.

Internal controls are designed, implemented and monitored to address identified business risk that threatens the achievement of any of the entity objectives regarding:

- Reliability of the financial reporting of the entity
- Effectiveness and efficiency of its operations
- Compliance with applicable laws and regulations

PCAOB AS 2201 is supplemented by AS 2601: *Consideration of an Entity's Use of a Service Organization* and AS 2605: *Consideration of the Internal Audit Function* in providing guidance for internal auditors who support the management assessment of the effectiveness of ICFR. It is important for internal auditors to understand these requirements and their relevance to designing and implementing internal controls to fulfill their own responsibilities and to provide oversight and support to others who support the management assessment of ICFR and the external audit opinion.

2.2 Sarbanes-Oxley Sections 302 and 404 Explained

The Sarbanes-Oxley Act was signed into law on July 30, 2002.[10] The law sought to fundamentally change the business and regulatory environment and "to enhance corporate responsibility, enhance financial disclosures and combat corporate and accounting fraud"[11] after the Enron bankruptcy and collapse of the Enron auditor Arthur Andersen. Among other provisions, Section 302 requires disclosure of internal controls. Section 404 provides for the assessment of internal controls.

Figure 2.1 provides summaries of Sections 302 and 404.

Figure 2.1—Sarbanes-Oxley Requirements Primer

	Section 302	Section 404
Who	Enterprise management, with the participation of the principal executive and financial officers (the certifying officers)	Corporate management, executives and financial officers (management has not been defined by the PCAOB)

[10] Sarbanes-Oxley Act of 2002, Public Law 107-204, 116 Stat. 745, 30 July 2002, *www.govinfo.gov/content/pkg/PLAW-107publ204/pdf/PLAW-107publ204.pdf*

[11] US Securities and Exchange Commission, "Investor Bulletin: An Introduction to The U.S. Securities and Exchange Commission – Rulemaking and Laws," 20 August 2015, *www.sec.gov/oiea/investor-alerts-bulletins/ib_rulemaking.html*

Figure 2.1—Sarbanes-Oxley Requirements Primer *(cont.)*

	Section 302	Section 404
What	1. Certifying officers are responsible for establishing and maintaining internal control over financial reporting. 2. Certifying officers have designed such internal control over financial reporting, or caused such internal control over financial reporting to be designed under their supervision, to provide reasonable assurance regarding the reliability of financial reporting and the preparation of financial statements for external purposes in accordance with generally accepted accounting principles. 3. Any changes in the enterprise's internal control over financial reporting that have occurred during the most recent fiscal quarter and have materially affected, or are reasonably likely to materially affect, the enterprise's internal control over financial reporting are disclosed. 4. When the reason for a change in internal control over financial reporting is the correction of a material weakness, management has a responsibility to determine whether the reason for the change and the circumstances surrounding that change are material information necessary to make the disclosure about the change not misleading.	1. A statement of management's responsibility for establishing and maintaining adequate internal control over financial reporting for the enterprise 2. A statement identifying the framework used by management to conduct the required assessment of the effectiveness of the enterprise's internal control over financial reporting 3. An assessment of the effectiveness of the enterprise's internal control over financial reporting as of the end of the most recent enterprise fiscal year, including an explicit statement whether internal control over financial reporting is effective 4. A statement that the registered public accounting firm that audited the financial statements included in the annual report has issued an attestation report on management's assessment of the enterprise's internal control over financial reporting 5. A written conclusion by management about the effectiveness of the enterprise's internal control over financial reporting is included in its report on internal control over financial reporting and in its representation letter to the auditor. The conclusion about the effectiveness of an enterprise's internal control over financial reporting can take many forms. However, management is required to state a direct conclusion about whether the enterprise's internal control over financial reporting is effective. 6. Management is precluded from concluding that the enterprise's internal control over financial reporting is effective if there are one or more material weaknesses. In addition, management is required to disclose all material weaknesses that exist as of the end of the most recent fiscal year.
How Often	Quarterly and annual assessment	Annual assessment by management and independent auditors

2.3 Key Requirements of Auditing Standard 2201

AS 2201[12] emphasizes that risk assessment is the foundation of the standard for auditing ICFR and for the way the external auditor assesses the management assessment of ICFR and the work of internal auditors and others. A risk-based approach governs the entire process, from the determination of significant accounts and disclosures and the relevant assertions to the selection of controls to test and the determination of the evidence necessary for a given control.

In particular, the standard emphasizes that a direct relationship exists between the degree of risk of a material weakness in internal controls over financial reporting and the amount of attention that will be devoted to that area by

[12] PCAOB, AS 2201: *An Audit of Internal Control Over Financial Reporting That Is Integrated with An Audit of Financial Statements*, PCAOB Release No. 2007-005A, *https://pcaobus.org/oversight/standards/auditing-standards/details/AS2201*

external auditors. Auditors will, therefore, focus on situations that present the strongest indicators that a material weakness in ICFR may exist.

AS 2605: *Consideration of the Internal Audit Function* establishes the requirements for the external auditor's assessment during the planning phase of the internal audit function and consideration of the use of the work of internal auditors. External auditors will consider the extent to which they can rely on internal audit when determining the nature, timing and extent of auditing procedures to be performed. That is because the internal audit function, when operating effectively, is an entity-level control similar to the audit committee. Ideally, internal audit serves as a control that monitors other controls.

When the auditor seeks to understand the major types of activities that the enterprise uses to monitor the effectiveness of its ICFR and how the enterprise initiates corrective actions related to its controls, the auditor may find that internal auditors or others performing an equivalent function contribute to the monitoring of controls. Paragraph .16 of AS 2201 describes how external auditors evaluate to what extent the work of others, including internal auditors, can be used to reduce the work that the auditor might otherwise perform.[13] Under the right circumstances, reliance on the work of internal auditors can reduce the length and cost of the audit without reducing its quality and effectiveness.

2.4 Defining Significant Deficiencies and Material Weaknesses

SEC rules require management and, therefore, its supporting functions such as internal audit, to base the evaluation of the effectiveness of the enterprise ICFR on a recognized control framework established by a body or group that followed due-process procedures, including the broad distribution of the framework for public comment. The most common framework used is from the COSO Internal Control – Integrated Framework report. The external auditor should use the same recognized control framework to perform his or her audit of ICFR as management uses for its annual evaluation of the effectiveness of the enterprise's ICFR.

The external auditor must plan and perform the audit with due professional care: "[D]ue professional care allows the auditor to obtain reasonable assurance about whether the financial statements are free of material misstatement, whether caused by error or fraud, or whether any material weaknesses exist as of the date of management's assessment."[14] If one or more material weaknesses exist, the enterprise internal control over financial reporting cannot be considered effective.[15] AS 2201 differentiates between significant deficiencies and material weaknesses in ICFR. A significant deficiency in ICFR is defined as:

> *...a deficiency, or a combination of deficiencies, in internal control over financial reporting that is less severe than a material weakness, yet important enough to merit attention by those responsible for oversight of the company's financial reporting.*[16]

A material weakness is defined as:

> *...a deficiency, or a combination of deficiencies, in internal control over financial reporting, such that there is a reasonable possibility that a material misstatement of the company's annual or interim financial statements will not be prevented or detected on a timely basis.*[17]

A material weakness in internal control over financial reporting may exist even when financial statements are not materially misstated. Strong indicators of a risk of a material weakness in ICFR include:

- Business units or transactions where senior management has identified fraud, whether or not material. Senior management in this case includes the principal executive and financial officers who sign the enterprise certifications, as required under Section 302 of SOX, and any other members of senior management who play a significant role in the company's financial reporting process.

[13] *Ibid.*
[14] PCAOB, AS 1015: *Due Professional Care in the Performance of Work*, *https://pcaobus.org/oversight/standards/auditing-standards/details/AS1015*
[15] 17 C.F.R. § 229.308, Item 308 of Regulation S-K, 1 April 2011, *www.govinfo.gov/content/pkg/CFR-2011-title17-vol2/pdf/CFR-2011-title17-vol2-sec229-308.pdf*
[16] *Op cit* PCAOB, AS 2201: *An Audit of Internal Control Over Financial Reporting That Is Integrated with An Audit of Financial Statements*
[17] *Ibid.*

- The decision to restate previously issued financial statements to reflect the correction of a material misstatement.
- The identification by the auditor of a material misstatement in the current period that would not have been detected by the enterprise internal control over financial reporting.
- Ineffective oversight of the enterprise's external financial reporting and internal control over financial reporting by the company's audit committee.

2.5 Audit Program

The following is an overview of the audit steps in completing the external audit of the effectiveness of ICFR:

1. Planning the Audit
    a. Obtain knowledge of the enterprise's internal controls over financial reporting.
    b. Become familiar with matters affecting the industry in which the enterprise operates, such as financial reporting practices, economic conditions, laws and regulations, and technological changes.
    c. Become familiar with matters relating to the enterprise's business model, including its organization, operating characteristics and capital structure, and any changes in these business model attributes that can affect its internal control over financial reporting.
    d. Develop preliminary judgments about materiality, risk and other factors relating to the determination of material weaknesses.
    e. Review control deficiencies previously communicated to the audit committee or management.
    f. Review legal or regulatory matters of which the enterprise is aware.
    g. Review the type and extent of available evidence related to the effectiveness of the enterprise's internal control over financial reporting and any preliminary assessment of the effectiveness of internal control over financial reporting.
    h. Review public information about the enterprise that is relevant to the evaluation of the likelihood of material financial statement misstatements and the effectiveness of the enterprise internal control over financial reporting.
    i. Review risk related to the enterprise that is evaluated as part of the auditor's client acceptance and retention evaluation.
    j. Assess the relative complexity of the enterprise operations.
2. Using a Top-Down Audit Approach
    a. Identify entity-level controls, including:
        i. Controls related to the control environment
        ii. Controls over management override
        iii. Enterprise risk assessment process
        iv. Centralized processing and controls, including shared service environments
        v. Controls to monitor results of operations
        vi. Controls to monitor other controls, including activities of the internal audit function, the audit committee and self-assessment programs
        vii. Controls over the period-end financial reporting process
        viii. Policies that address significant business control and risk management practices

b. Identify IT general controls including general controls over program changes, access to programs and computer operations.

c. Identify application controls, including controls built into software on which management relies to achieve its control objectives and the IT general controls that are important to the effective operation of those application controls.

d. Understand how IT affects the flow of transactions in the enterprise. See AS 2110: *Identifying and Assessing Risks of Material Misstatement*, paragraph 29, and Appendix B, which discuss the effect of information technology on ICFR and the risk to assess.[18]

e. Identify significant accounts and disclosures and their relevant assertions. The financial statement assertions include:

    i. Existence or occurrence

    ii. Completeness

    iii. Valuation or allocation

    iv. Rights and obligations

    v. Presentation and disclosure

f. Understand likely sources of misstatement.

g. Understand the flow of transactions related to the relevant assertions, including how these transactions are initiated, authorized, processed and recorded.

h. Verify the points within the enterprise processes at which a misstatement—including a misstatement due to fraud—can arise that, individually or in combination with other misstatements, would be material.

i. Identify the controls that management has implemented to address these potential misstatements.

j. Identify the controls that management has implemented over the prevention or timely detection of unauthorized acquisition, use or disposition of the enterprise assets that can result in a material misstatement of the financial statements.

k. Select controls to test.

3. Testing Controls

    a. Consider the prior-year audit reports.

    b. Test design effectiveness.

    c. Test operating effectiveness.

    d. Relate risk to the evidence to be obtained during testing.

4. Evaluating Identified Deficiencies

    a. Evaluate the severity of control deficiencies.

    b. Evaluate whether control deficiencies, individually or collectively, rise to the level of significant deficiencies or material weaknesses.

5. Wrapping Up the Audit

6. Writing the Audit Opinion

    a. Obtain written management representations.

    b. Communicate matters to management and the audit committee.

7. Reporting on Internal Control

    a. Issue a report with the auditor's opinion.

    b. Report any material weaknesses.

    c. Review for subsequent events.

[18] *Ibid.*

2.6 Role of Risk Assessments

Risk assessments are fundamental to performing SOX-related audits and are the foundation of everything prescribed in AS 2201. The risk assessment influences many aspects of the audit plan and execution:

- Determination of significant accounts and disclosures and relevant assertions
- Selection of controls to test
- Determination of the evidence necessary to testing for a given control

AS 2110: *Identifying and Assessing Risks of Material Misstatement* establishes requirements regarding the process of identifying and assessing risk of material misstatement of the financial statements. The auditor identifies and assesses the risk of material misstatement at the financial statement level and the assertion level.

Understanding the enterprise's control environment—including the policies and actions of management, the board and the audit committee concerning the enterprise's control environment—and understanding of relevant industry, regulatory and other factors are critical to assessing the level of risk of material misstatement due to error or fraud. The risk assessment can assist auditors in obtaining an understanding of the management process for identifying risk relevant to financial reporting objectives, including risk of material misstatement due to fraud.

According to AS 2110, paragraph .52, any discussion among audit team members about the potential for material misstatement due to fraud should "occur with an attitude that includes a questioning mind, and the key engagement team members should set aside any prior beliefs they might have that management is honest and has integrity."[19] Paragraph .65 directs auditors to review the risk assessment procedures performed to determine whether all the information gathered would indicate that one or more fraud risk factors are present and should be considered in identifying and assessing fraud risk.[20]

Internal auditors should provide external auditors with any insight they have regarding enterprise fraud risk and whether the internal auditors have knowledge of fraud, alleged fraud or suspected fraud that would affect the enterprise's financial statements. External auditors also want to know whether management has satisfactorily responded to any findings by internal auditors who have performed any procedures to identify or detect fraud during the year. Finally, external auditors ask internal auditors if they are aware of instances of management override of controls and whether the enterprise has any significant unusual transactions.

The organization overall control environment, or tone at the top, has a significant impact on the internal controls over the enterprise information system, including the related business processes relevant to financial reporting. Those controls also dictate how the information system captures events and conditions, other than transactions, that are significant to the financial statements. The external and internal auditor must obtain an understanding of the extent of manual controls and automated controls used by the enterprise, including the IT general controls that are important to the effective operation of automated controls.

AS 2601: *Consideration of an Entity's Use of a Service Organization* addresses the auditor's responsibilities for obtaining an understanding of controls at a third-party service organization that are part of the enterprise information system over financial reporting. AS 2601 is discussed in more detail in Chapter 5.

Examples of IT-related specific risk to enterprise internal control over financial reporting include:[21]

- Reliance on systems or programs that are inaccurately processing data, processing inaccurate data or both

[19] PCAOB, AS 2110: *Identifying and Assessing Risks of Material Misstatement*, PCAOB Release No. 2010-004, *https://pcaobus.org/oversight/standards/auditing-standards/details/AS2110*

[20] *Ibid.*

[21] *Ibid.*

- Unauthorized access to data that might result in destruction of data or improper changes to data, including the recording of unauthorized or nonexistent transactions, or inaccurate recording of transactions. Risk items might arise when multiple users access a common database.
- The possibility of IT personnel gaining access privileges beyond those necessary to perform their assigned duties, thereby breaking down segregation of duties
- Unauthorized changes to data in master files
- Unauthorized changes to systems or programs
- Failure to make necessary changes to systems or programs
- Inappropriate manual intervention
- Potential loss of data or inability to access data as required

2.7 Identifying Entity-Level Controls

AS 2201 places considerable emphasis on entity-level controls. The standard notes the following:

> *The auditor must test those entity-level controls that are important to the auditor's conclusion about whether the company has effective internal control over financial reporting. The auditor's evaluation of entity-level controls can result in increasing or decreasing the testing that the auditor otherwise would have performed on other controls.*[22]

Entity-level controls include, but are not limited to:

- Controls related to the overall control environment
- Controls over management override
- Enterprise risk assessment process
- Centralized processing and controls, including shared service environments
- Controls to monitor results of operations
- Controls to monitor other controls, including activities of the internal audit function, the audit committee and self-assessment programs
- Controls over the period-end financial reporting process
- Policies that address significant business control and risk management practices

AS 2201 affirms that controls over management overrides are important for all enterprises. However, controls over management overrides may be particularly important at smaller enterprises because senior management can be directly involved in the period-end financial accounting and reporting process and in performing controls over these processes. The controls that must be in place in a smaller company to address the risk of management overrides might, therefore, be different from those in larger enterprises.

Many entity-level controls have IT implications. For example, COBIT 2019 practices APO02.01 *Understand enterprise context and direction*, APO02.02 *Assess current capabilities, performance and digital maturity of the enterprise*, APO02.03 *Define target digital capabilities*, and APO02.04 *Conduct a gap analysis* provide a holistic view of the business and its IT environment, where the firm is on the digital maturity spectrum, and the target capabilities required to migrate to a future environment. Technology migration plans leverage infrastructure and architecture—including externally provided services and related capabilities—in a controlled manner to enable nimble, reliable and efficient responses to strategic business objectives.

[22] *Op cit* PCAOB, AS 2201: *An Audit of Internal Control Over Financial Reporting That Is Integrated with An Audit of Financial Statements*

2.8 Identifying Information Technology General Controls (ITGC)

Information technology general controls (ITGCs) are described in PCAOB standards as general controls that relate to the overall IT environment, rather than specific applications, and support the effective functioning of specific application controls by helping to ensure the continued timely, reliable, accurate and authorized operation of information systems. General controls commonly include controls over data center and network operations; system software acquisition and maintenance, including change controls over application updates and patches; access security; and application software acquisition, development, tracking and maintenance.

ITGCs are entity-level controls because they are the centralized processing and centralized controls that support all other automated controls, including in shared services environments. These entity-level controls are critical to the auditor's assessment of whether the enterprise has effective ICFR, because they may have an important, but indirect, effect on the likelihood that a misstatement will be detected or prevented on a timely basis. Because ITGCs often monitor the effectiveness of other controls, the level and extent of ITGC effectiveness also impacts the external auditor's selection of other controls for testing and the nature, timing and extent of procedures that the auditor performs on those controls.

2.9 Identifying Application Controls

Application controls are specific to each software application and refer to the controls over individual automated business processes, including data edits, separation of business functions, balancing of processing totals, transaction logging and error reporting. AS 2201 establishes a foundational assumption that entirely automated application controls are generally not subject to breakdowns due to human failure. Human error or manipulation does not usually impact an automated control when relevant ITGCs are effective.

AS 2201, therefore, allows the auditor to use a benchmarking strategy for assessing automated application controls. The standard describes the benchmarking strategy as follows:

> *If general controls over program changes, access to programs, and computer operations are effective and continue to be tested, and if the auditor verifies that the automated application control has not changed since the auditor established a baseline (i.e., last tested the application control), the auditor may conclude that the automated application control continues to be effective without repeating the prior year's specific tests of the operation of the automated application control. The nature and extent of the evidence that the auditor should obtain to verify that the control has not changed may vary depending on the circumstances, including depending on the strength of the company's program change controls.*[23]

According to AS 2201, the auditor should evaluate the following factors to determine when to re-establish a baseline for the benchmarking approach:[24]

- Effectiveness of the IT control environment, including controls over application and system software acquisition and maintenance, access controls and computer operations
- Auditor's understanding of the nature of changes, if any, on the specific programs that contain the controls
- Nature and timing of other related tests
- Consequences of errors associated with the application control that was benchmarked
- Sensitivity of the control to other business factors that may have changed (for example, an automated control may have been designed with the assumption that only positive amounts will exist in a file; such a control is no longer effective if negative amounts, credits, begin to be posted to the account)

[23] PCAOB, AS 2201: *An Audit of Internal Control Over Financial Reporting That Is Integrated with An Audit of Financial Statements*, Appendix B, PCAOB Release No. 2007-005A, *https://pcaobus.org/oversight/standards/auditing-standards/details/AS2201*

[24] *Ibid.*

Application controls are discussed in detail in Chapter 4 of this publication.

2.10 Addressing the Risk of Fraud

AS 2201 gives considerable emphasis to fraud assessment and controls for fraud prevention and detection. AS 2201 requires that the results of a fraud risk assessment must be considered when planning and performing the audit of internal control over financial reporting.[25]

When identifying and testing entity-level controls and selecting other controls to test, the external auditor should evaluate whether the enterprise's ICFR sufficiently addresses identified risk of material misstatement due to fraud and includes controls intended to address the risk of management override of other controls.[26]

Many fraud-related controls have IT implications. For example, AS 2201 pays particular attention to journal entries and adjustments that are processed through partially automated or fully automated ERP software.[27] Fraud can also occur when ITGCs, such as access controls, are weak, because that may allow someone to change data directly at the database level rather than through automated workflows that have authorization and edit controls and produce audit trail reports of activity. Effective ITGCs and accounting and financial reporting software application controls can make fraud that relies on manipulating journal entries and transaction data easier to prevent and detect.

Smaller, less complex enterprises may have a mix of manual and automated systems and use tools, such as spreadsheets, to create data that feed into the general ledger. Manual processes that work with or alongside automated systems may not have the same built-in controls, such as access, authorization and segregation of duties, as automated systems. Both internal and external auditors should keep in mind the source of data in the destination automated systems and the potential for corruption or manipulation of data via less controlled initial and intermediate processes. There may be alternative compensating controls to achieve control objectives, but the internal and external auditor must evaluate the design and effectiveness of the controls over subsidiary manual systems if they feed automated systems.

Finally, when auditing internal control over financial reporting, auditors may become aware of fraud or possible illegal acts related to IT. In such circumstances, external auditors must determine their responsibilities under AS 2401: *Consideration of Fraud in a Financial Statement Audit*, AS 2405: *Illegal Acts by Clients* and Section 10A of the Securities Exchange Act of 1934. Internal auditors also have corporate, legal and ethical obligations to escalate evidence of fraud or illegal acts within the organization and, perhaps, outside the organization to regulators or other law enforcement authorities. Internal auditors also may assist with or cooperate in internal and external investigations of suspected fraud or illegal acts.

When IT-related risk is not incorporated into the risk assessment process, the external auditor is taking a chance that IT-related control weaknesses may cause ICFR weaknesses. Lapses or circumvention of security, access or change management procedures and cybervulnerabilities reflect pervasive IT risk that can impact operations performance and the integrity of financial reporting.

2.11 Special Considerations for Emerging Growth Companies (EGCs)

Auditor opinions on internal controls over financial reporting are required for most larger public enterprises under Section 404(b) of the Sarbanes-Oxley Act of 2002. Enterprises with less than US $75 million in public float are permanently exempted from the auditors' ICFR opinion. Enterprises that are not exempt are not required to have their first auditor's opinion on ICFR until their second year as a public enterprise.

[25] *Ibid.*
[26] *Ibid.*
[27] *Ibid.*

The Jumpstart Our Business Startups (JOBS) Act, passed by the US Congress in April 2012, generally provides that new PCAOB standards do not apply to the audits of emerging growth companies (EGCs) unless the SEC determines that applying such additional requirements is necessary or appropriate in the public interest, after considering the protection of investors, and whether the action will promote efficiency, competition and capital formation.[28]

When the JOBS Act was passed, it created the designation of an emerging growth company. EGCs are exempt from the requirement to obtain an auditor's opinion on ICFR for up to five years, or until they exceed US $1.07 billion in revenue. At the time the JOBS Act was passed, it exempted enterprises that have total annual gross revenue of less than US $1.07 billion from having to obtain the auditor's opinion on ICFR. An enterprise continues to be an emerging growth company for the first five fiscal years after it completes an initial public offering (IPO), unless one of the following occurs:

- Its total annual gross revenues are US $1.07 billion or more.
- It issued more than US $1 billion in nonconvertible debt in the past three years.
- It becomes a large accelerated filer, per SEC rules.

In March 2020, the SEC approved an amendment that changed the definitions for enterprises required to file with the regulator.[29] One impact of the change is that smaller reporting enterprises with less than US $100 million in revenues are no longer required to obtain a separate attestation of their ICFR from an outside auditor. These enterprises continue to be required to establish and maintain effective ICFR, and their principal executive and financial officers must continue to certify that, among other things, they are responsible for establishing and maintaining ICFR and have evaluated and reported on the effectiveness of the enterprise disclosure controls and procedures.

As of June 5, 2021, according to data from research firm Audit Analytics, there are 2,116 EGCs, but the increase in EGCs from the end of 2019[30] is almost totally attributable to an increase in blank check enterprises.[31] Special purpose acquisition companies (SPACs) are a type of blank check enterprise. A SPAC raises capital in the public markets with the sole intention of identifying and merging with a target, a private operating enterprise. SPACs have become more popular for various transactions since the beginning of 2020, including for transitioning an enterprise from a private enterprise to a publicly traded enterprise.

Blank check enterprises are typically development stage enterprises that have no revenue, no specific business plan or purpose, or have indicated that their business plan is to engage in a merger or acquisition with an unidentified enterprise or enterprises, other entity, or person. These enterprises typically involve speculative investments and often fall within the SEC definition of penny stocks or are considered microcap stocks.

On March 31, 2020, the SEC acting chief accountant issued a warning to SPAC sponsors, target enterprises and potential investors, stating the following:

> *The combined public company should have personnel and processes in place to produce high quality financial reporting that is in compliance with all SEC rules and regulations. Among other considerations, the combined public company should have finance and accounting professionals with sufficient knowledge of the relevant reporting requirements, including the applicable accounting requirements, and the appropriate staffing to meet deadlines for required current and periodic reports.*[32]

[28] US Government Printing Office, "Jumpstart Our Business Startups Act," Public Law 112-106, 112th Congress, Page 126 STAT. 306, 5 April 2012, *www.govinfo.gov/content/pkg/PLAW-112publ106/html/PLAW-112publ106.htm*

[29] US Securities and Exchange Commission, "Accelerated Filer and Large Accelerated Filer Definitions: SEC Final Rule," 17 CFR Parts 229, 230, 240, and 249, Release No. 34-88365; File No. S7-06-19, 12 March 2020, *www.sec.gov/rules/final/2020/34-88365.pdf*

[30] Data as of 15 June 2001 were provided directly to the author by D. Coleman of Audit Analytics®. Data as of 2019 are based on the PCAOB's latest report in November 2020 for EGC status as of 15 November 2019; see ElRafey, A.; K. Poy; H. Samaraweera; "Characteristics of Emerging Growth Companies and Their Audit Firms as of November 15, 2019," PCAOB, November 2020, *https://pcaob-assets.azureedge.net/pcaob-dev/docs/default-source/economicandriskanalysis/projectsother/documents/white-paper-characteristics-emerging-growth-companies-november-15-2019.pdf?sfvrsn=fc2412dd_2*. Additional data provided by Coleman, D.; "Updated Report on Emerging Growth Companies," 25 May 2017, *https://blog.auditanalytics.com/updated-report-on-emerging-growth-companies/*

[31] *Op cit* ElRafey, A., *et al.*

[32] Munter, P.; "Financial Reporting and Auditing Considerations of Companies Merging with SPACs," US Securities and Exchange Commission Public Statement," 31 March 2021, *www.sec.gov/news/public-statement/munter-spac-20200331*

The acting chief accountant also emphasized in the message that it is important for target enterprises to understand ICFR, disclosure controls and procedure requirements and have a plan in place for the combined public enterprise to comply with those requirements on a timely basis. SPAC management is required under Section 404(a) of the Sarbanes-Oxley Act, to conduct an annual evaluation of the enterprise ICFR, just like any other enterprise.[33] It is important for management and internal auditors to understand the timing of when the first annual ICFR assessment is required and whether an auditor's report on ICFR is required under Section 404(b) of SOX. For some situations, the SEC may not object to the exclusion of an annual ICFR assessment for an enterprise.[34]

2.12 Special Considerations Regarding ICFR and Cybersecurity Risk

Regulators and audit industry organizations have taken several actions to respond to continued cybersecurity threats to their regulated organizations. For example, the AICPA and its Center for Audit Quality (CAQ) published resources for audit committees and auditors. The CAQ recommended in 2018 that board members have a conversation with external auditors about cybersecurity.[35] The purpose of the CAQ's guideline document is to clarify the "current roles and responsibilities of the financial statement auditor when it comes to cybersecurity." The conversation clarifying roles and responsibilities may include, if applicable, a discussion of the audit of the effectiveness of the enterprise ICFR.

However, the CAQ guideline document and subsequent publications make the audit industry's position on cybersecurity and the scope of the audit very clear: The cybersecurity risk management practices of an enterprise are typically beyond the scope of a typical financial statement audit.[36] However, the CAQ, speaking for the external auditors of public enterprises, wants enterprises to consider the external auditors as the best qualified consultants to deliver cybersecurity risk assessment and risk management services. An AICPA® cybersecurity resource center provides guidance to help organizations and businesses, including certified public accounting (CPA) firms, assess cybersecurity risk.[37] The AICPA published a new attest guide and resource page to assist certified public accountants (CPAs) who are engaged to examine and report on the cybersecurity risk management program of an entity.

In April 2018, the US National Institute of Standards and Technology (NIST) released a revised version of its widely used *Framework for Improving Critical Infrastructure Cybersecurity*, a voluntary framework for reducing cyberrisk to critical infrastructure. The NIST framework provides an approach to prioritize cybersecurity resources, make risk decisions and take action to reduce risk.[38]

The SEC has made it clear that whether enterprises seek assistance from external auditors, internal auditors, third-party consultants or some combination of all three, it is "critical that public companies take all required actions to inform investors about material cybersecurity risks and incidents in a timely fashion, including those companies that are subject to material cybersecurity risks but may not yet have been the target of a cyber-attack."[39]

[33] US Government Publishing Office, "Public Law 107-204, 107th Congress," 116 Stat. 745, 30 July 2002, Securities Exchange Act of 1934, Rules 13a-15(c) and 15d-15(c), *www.govinfo.gov/content/pkg/PLAW-107publ204/pdf/PLAW-107publ204.pdf*

[34] For instances where the SEC staff would not object if the issuer excludes the management assessment of ICFR from the Form 10-K, and the disclosures that should be included in the report, see U.S. Securities and Exchange Commission, "Regulation S-K: Questions and Answers of General Applicability," 215.0,21 September 2020, *www.sec.gov/divisions/corpfin/guidance/regs-kinterp.htm.*

[35] CAQ Center for Audit Quality, "Cybersecurity Risk Management Oversight: A Tool for Board Members," 12 April 2018, *www.thecaq.org/cybersecurity-risk-management-oversight-tool-board-members/*

[36] Fornelli, C.; "Talk to Your Auditors About Cybersecurity," NACD Boardtalk, 8 May 2018, *https://blog.nacdonline.org/posts/talk-to-auditors-cybersecurity*

[37] AICPA, "Cybersecurity Resource Center,"https://us.aicpa.org/interestareas/frc/assuranceadvisoryservices/cyber-security-resource-center

[38] NIST, "NIST Releases Version 1.1 of Its Popular Cybersecurity Framework," 16 April 2018, *www.nist.gov/news-events/news/2018/04/nist-releases-version-11-its-popular-cybersecurity-framework*

[39] US Securities and Exchange Commission, "Commission Statement and Guidance on Public Company Cybersecurity Disclosures, Securities Act," 17 CFR Parts 229 and 249, Release Nos. 33-10459; 34-82746, 21 February 2018, *www.sec.gov/rules/interp/2018/33-10459.pdf*

In February 2018, the SEC published guidance to help public enterprises prepare disclosures about cybersecurity risk and incidents.[40] This guidance emphasizes the importance for public enterprises to maintain comprehensive policies and procedures related to cybersecurity risk and incidents.

The SEC guidance describes how enterprises generally weigh, among other things, the potential materiality of any identified cybersecurity risk and, in the case of incidents, the importance of any compromised information and of the impact when determining which, if any, disclosures to make in the financial statements or the footnotes. Enterprises should disclose cybersecurity risk and incidents that are material (i.e., there is a substantial likelihood that a reasonable investor would consider the information important in making an investment decision or that disclosure of the omitted information would have been viewed by the reasonable investor as having significantly altered the total mix of information available).[41]

SEC guidance explains that the materiality of cybersecurity risk or incidents depends on their:

> *...nature, extent, and potential magnitude, particularly as they relate to any compromised information or the business and scope of company operations.*
> *The materiality of cybersecurity risks and incidents also depends on the range of harm that such incidents could cause. This includes harm to a company's reputation, financial performance, and customer and vendor relationships, as well as the possibility of litigation or regulatory investigations or actions, including regulatory actions by state and federal governmental authorities and non-U.S. authorities.*[42]

The PCAOB monitors developments related to cybersecurity and considers an auditor's response to a cyber incident at a client enterprise during PCAOB inspection and enforcement activities.[43]

PCAOB standards require auditors to obtain an understanding of how the enterprise uses information technology and how IT affects the flow of transactions in business processes. The auditor must also gain an understanding of the specific risk to the enterprise internal control over financial reporting resulting from IT, including unauthorized changes to systems, programs or data in master files and potential loss of data or inability to access data as required.[44]

PCAOB inspections staff review and develop an understanding of how firms evaluate the risk of material misstatement associated with cybersecurity and any impact to the related ICFR and financial statements.[45] Cyberattacks may affect issuer financial statement reporting, and, as a result, PCAOB inspections staff view this as a risk area that requires ongoing focus by external auditors.

CPAs can serve clients with cybersecurity risk needs via a voluntary framework developed by the AICPA— System and Organizational Controls (SOC) for Cybersecurity.[46] This framework is discussed in Chapter 5 of this publication.

[40] US Securities and Exchange Commission, "Commission Statement and Guidance on Public Company Cybersecurity Disclosures, Securities Act," 17 CFR Parts 229 and 249, Release Nos. 33-10459; 34-82746, 21 February 2018, *www.sec.gov/rules/interp/2018/33-10459.pdf*

[41] This approach is consistent with the standard of materiality articulated by the US Supreme Court in *TSC Industries v. Northway*, 426 U.S. 438, 449 (1976), as follows: A fact is material "if there is a substantial likelihood that a reasonable shareholder would consider it important" in making an investment decision or if it "would have been viewed by the reasonable investor as having significantly altered the 'total mix' of information made available" to the shareholder.

[42] US Securities and Exchange Commission, "Commission Statement and Guidance on Public Company Cybersecurity Disclosures, Securities Act," 17 CFR Parts 229 and 249, Release Nos. 33-10459; 34-82746, 21 February 2018, *www.sec.gov/rules/interp/2018/33-10459.pdf*

[43] PCAOB, Standing Advisory Group Meeting: Panel Discussion – Cybersecurity, 5-6 June 2018, *https://pcaob-assets.azureedge.net/pcaob-dev/docs/default-source/news/events/documents/cybersecurity-briefing-paper.pdf*

[44] *Op cit* PCAOB, AS 2110: *Identifying and Assessing Risks of Material Misstatement*, Appendix B

[45] PCAOB, "PCAOB Publishes Staff Inspection Brief Previewing 2016 Inspection Findings," 10 November 2017, *https://pcaobus.org/news-events/news-releases/news-release-detail/pcaob-publishes-staff-inspection-brief-previewing-2016-inspection-findings_641*

[46] AICPA, "SOC for Cybersecurity," *www.aicpa.org/interestareas/frc/assuranceadvisoryservices/aicpacybersecurityinitiative.html*

2.13 Special Considerations for ICFR Audits in a Cloud Computing Environment

NIST defines cloud computing as a means for enabling on-demand access to shared pools of configurable computing resources (e.g., networks, servers, storage applications and services) that can be rapidly provisioned and released.[47]

Storing data, conducting business and communicating using the cloud increases existing risk and creates new and potentially unfamiliar risk. Operating in a cloud environment forces enterprises and their internal and external auditors to rethink corporate and IT governance, risk management, privacy, change management, cybersecurity, internal audit and external assurance, among many other areas of business activity.

Cloud services can come in many shapes and forms—private cloud, public cloud, hybrid cloud or community cloud deployment. The business/payment model for cloud vendors also varies from Infrastructure as a Service (IaaS), Software as a Service (SaaS) and Platform as a Service (PaaS) to pay-as-you-go models.

The COVID-19 pandemic resulted in businesses and workers suddenly, and sometimes haphazardly, transitioning to remote working. That transformation was made possible, in part, by cloud computing. Data, software and applications are now readily available from the bedroom to the kitchen and from the beach house to the boat. However, many enterprises were forced to operate remotely and more virtually and may have been ill-prepared, thereby increasing existing risk and creating new risk.

The PCAOB noted in a bulletin issued in December 2020 that the COVID-19 pandemic introduced changes in the business environment that may have affected certain processes, the flow of transactions and the related controls over financial reporting. For example, furloughs, new technologies and other workforce changes may have necessitated reassigning internal control owners and designing workarounds to provide alternative ways of completing key business processes and internal control activities. A public enterprise response to the pandemic may have also affected the operation of IT-related controls and monitoring or review-type controls.

These changes influence the internal and external auditors' understanding and evaluation of ICFR. Changes to the operation of relevant controls may have been thought to be only temporary, but, in many cases, may become permanent. This may affect the auditors' approaches to selecting controls to test and the nature, timing and extent of procedures performed to support the ICFR assessment and opinion, and the external auditor's control reliance strategy in the financial statement audit. Changes to the frequency of the performance of certain controls, including whether the operation of controls has been affected by business disruptions, may inform the timing and extent of the auditor's tests of operating effectiveness.[48]

In addition to these changes, the influence of cloud computing should also be considered. The Cloud Security Alliance® (CSA), a not-for-profit, member-driven organization dedicated to defining and raising awareness of best practices to help ensure a secure cloud computing environment, put together a "Top Threats from Cloud Computing" report in 2019.[49] The threats, risk and vulnerabilities in the cloud are often the result of the shared, on-demand nature of cloud computing. Their egregious eleven threats ranked in order of significance follow:

1. Data breaches
2. Misconfiguration and inadequate change control
3. Lack of cloud security architecture and strategy
4. Insufficient identity, credential, access and key management
5. Account hijacking

[47] Mell, P.; T. Grance; "The NIST Definition of Cloud Computing," Special Publication 800-145, NIST, 21 September 2011, *https://nvlpubs.nist.gov/nistpubs/Legacy/SP/nistspecialpublication800-145.pdf*

[48] PCAOB, "Staff Observations and Reminders during the COVID-19 Pandemic," December 2020, *Spotlight*, *https://pcaob-assets.azureedge.net/pcaob-dev/docs/default-source/documents/staff-observations-reminders-covid-19-spotlight.pdf?sfvrsn=b14c0d8_6*

[49] CSA, "Top Threats to Cloud Computing: The Egregious 11," 6 August 2019, *https://cloudsecurityalliance.org/artifacts/top-threats-to-cloud-computing-egregious-eleven/*

6. Insider threat
7. Insecure interfaces and application programming interfaces (APIs)
8. Weak control plane
9. Metastructure and applistructure failures
10. Limited cloud usage visibility
11. Abuse and nefarious use of cloud services

2.14 Special Considerations for ICFR Audits of Brokers and Dealers

The Dodd-Frank Wall Street Reform and Consumer Protection Act of 2010[50] expanded the authority of the PCAOB to oversee the audits of brokers and dealers that are required under SEC rules, even if they are not publicly listed on an exchange. On July 30, 2013, the SEC amended its rules, including SEC Rule 17a-5 under the Exchange Act, to require, among other things, that audits of broker-dealer financial statements and examinations of reports regarding compliance with SEC requirements be performed in accordance with PCAOB auditing standards, effective for fiscal years ending on or after June 1, 2014.[51]

2.15 Where to Find IT Controls

It is necessary to consider at least three elements when seeking to understand the locations of IT controls in the typical enterprise. **Figure 2.2** illustrates the common elements of enterprises.

[50] Dodd-Frank Wall Street Reform and Consumer Protection Act, Public Law 111-203, 21 July 2010, *www.congress.gov/bill/111th-congress/house-bill/4173/text*

[51] US Securities and Exchange Commission, "Broker-Dealer Report," 17 CFR Parts 240 and 249, Release No. 34-70073; File No. S7-23-11, 30 July 2013, *www.sec.gov/rules/final/2013/34-70073.pdf*

Figure 2.2—Common Elements of Enterprise

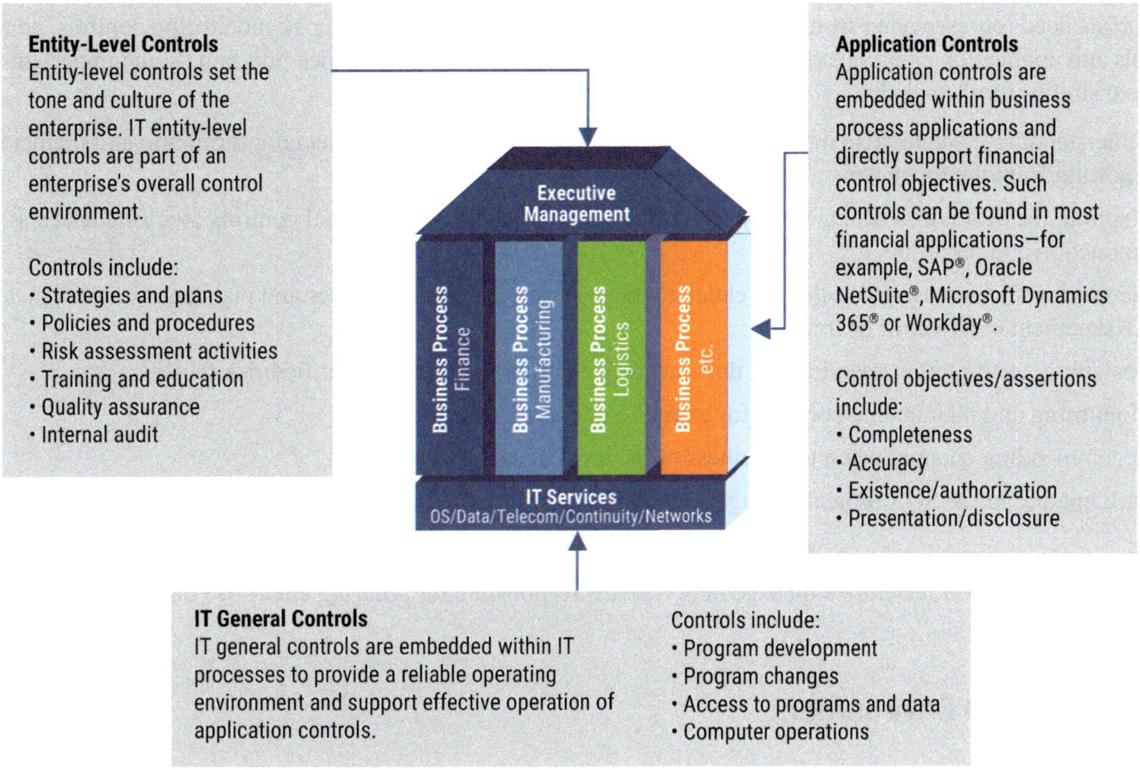

Source: Adapted from ISACA, *IT Control Objectives for Sarbanes-Oxley: Using COBIT® 5 in the Design and Implementation of Internal Controls Over Financial Reporting, 3rd Edition*, USA, 2014, *https://store.isaca.org/s/store#/store/browse/detail/a2S4w000004Ko9JEAS*

2.16 Using the Work of Others

AS 2605 *Consideration of the Internal Audit Function* governs how the external auditor evaluates the extent to which the work of others is relied upon. The purpose is to reduce the work that the external auditor performs. The standard provides guidance for how the external auditor evaluates the quality and effectiveness of the internal audit function's work, not only as a potential source of support, but also as a critical entity-level control when planning the audit. The extent of these procedures depends on how much of the internal auditors' work may affect the external auditor's procedures for significant account balances or classes of transactions.

As discussed earlier, reliance by external auditors on the work of internal auditors can reduce the length and cost of the audit without reducing its quality and effectiveness. Internal audit provides a base to external audit with analysis, evaluations and broader control testing activities. If tuned in a better way, internal audit can have a key role even in ITGC testing. This provides a greater opportunity for the management to keep the overall program under control.

2.17 Information Systems and Technology Controls

The Sarbanes-Oxley Act makes corporate executives explicitly responsible for establishing, evaluating and monitoring the effectiveness of ICFR. For most enterprises, the role of IT is crucial to achieve this objective.

Whether through a unified enterprise resource planning (ERP) system or a disparate collection of operational and financial management software applications, IT is the foundation of an effective system of ICFR in the modern organization.

Enterprises need representation from IT on their SOX teams to determine whether IT monitoring controls, general controls and application controls exist and support the objectives of the compliance program. Some important areas of responsibility for IT include:

- Understanding the enterprise internal control program for production of financial information and financial reporting from the top down
- Mapping the IT environment (IT services and processes) that supports internal controls over financial statement production and reporting
- Identifying and assessing risk that is related to these IT services and processes and that can result in a material misstatement due to error or fraud
- Designing, testing, implementing and documenting controls to mitigate identified risk factors
- Monitoring and maintaining controls for effective operation over time
- Recommending changes when the business or business needs change
- Participating in the SOX project management office

In outsourced or shared service models, enterprises may rely on their cloud providers for secure data centers and infrastructure. However, enterprise management remains responsible for securing enterprise data and applications in the cloud.

2.18 IT Control Environment

The IT control environment relates to the entity-level controls defined by AS 2201. This environment includes the IT governance process, monitoring and reporting. The IT governance process includes information systems strategic planning; the IT risk management process; compliance and regulatory management; and IT policies, procedures and standards. Monitoring and reporting are required to align IT with business requirements.

The IT governance structure should be designed so that IT adds value to the business and IT risk factors are addressed. This governance structure also includes an IT organization structure that supports and promotes the achievement of the enterprise objectives.

2.19 Computer Operations

These include controls over the definition, acquisition, installation, configuration, integration and maintenance of the IT infrastructure. Ongoing controls over operations address the day-to-day delivery of information services, including service-level management, management of third-party services, system availability, customer relationship management, configuration and systems management, problem and incident management, operations management scheduling, and facilities management.

The system software component of operations includes controls over the effective acquisition, implementation, configuration and maintenance of operating system software, database management systems, middleware software, communications software, security software, and utilities that run the system and allow applications to function. System software also provides the incident tracking, system logging and monitoring functions. System software can report on users of database utilities and other utility functions. If someone accesses these powerful data-altering functions, that individual's use is recorded and reported for review.

2.20 Access to Programs and Data

The objective of access to programs and data (or managed access) processes is to provide access to the IT environment (e.g., IT applications, databases, operating systems, network software and tools) only to authorized, appropriate users who are restricted to performing authorized, appropriate actions. The authentication path provides relevant information about which IT environment components are relevant to the financial statements. The access to programs and data processes includes establishment and maintenance of appropriate security settings for IT environment components relevant to the audit and the administration of related access rights to, and within, the IT environment.

Access controls over programs and data assume greater importance as internal and external connectivity to entity networks grows. Internal users may be halfway around the world or down the hall, and there may be thousands of external users accessing, or trying to access, entity systems. Effective access security controls can provide a reasonable level of assurance against inappropriate access and unauthorized use of systems. If designed well, they can intercept unethical hackers, malicious software and other intrusion attempts.

Adequate access control activities, such as secure passwords, Internet firewalls, data encryption and cryptographic keys, can be effective methods of preventing unauthorized access. User accounts and related access privilege controls restrict the applications or application functions only to authorized users that need them to do their jobs, supporting an appropriate segregation of duties.

Review of the user profiles (user and shared accounts) that permit or restrict access should be frequent and timely. Similarly, profiles of individuals who know the passwords for shared accounts are required to be reviewed. Former or disgruntled employees can be a threat to a system; therefore, terminated employee passwords and user IDs should be revoked immediately. By preventing unauthorized use of, and changes to, the system, an entity protects its data and program integrity.

2.21 Program Development and Change Management

Application software development and maintenance have two principal components—the acquisition and implementation of new applications and the maintenance of existing applications. The acquisition and implementation process for new applications is a very high-risk activity and frequently results in schedule and budget overruns if not actual failure. Entities should select the appropriate system development and quality assurance (QA) methodology to reduce software acquisition, development and implementation risk.

The choice of approach to software acquisition, development and implementation, whether in-house or by a vendor, should be focused on project criticality and the ability of the organization to respond to change. Most enterprises use either a heavyweight, traditional waterfall methodology or a lightweight agile modeling methodology. The traditional approach to software development and implementation incorporates comprehensive planning, detailed documentation and robust design. Standard software tools and IT architecture components often support this methodology. Agile methodologies take advantage of short iterative cycles to produce usable code and processes and rely more heavily on shared knowledge and constant communication than formal documentation. Agile methods allow applications to be built quickly without extensive quality assurance phases.

However, development of applications that are mission critical and require high reliability and data integrity is typically better suited to a traditional software development life cycle (SDLC) approach. If an application is mission critical, requirements must be well defined before the software is coded; otherwise, unexpected and undetected defects may haunt the process. An agile method can be highly effective in handling subsequent changes, because constant feedback from users or customers is easily addressed via the short, iterative development life cycle.

Ongoing change management and the implementation of new releases of software are addressed via application maintenance activities. Appropriate controls over changes to the system should exist so that all changes are made properly. The extent of testing that is required for the new release of a system should also be determined. For example, the implementation of a major new software release may require the evaluation of enhancements to the system, extensive testing, user retraining and rewriting of procedures. Controls may involve required authorization of change requests; review of the changes, approvals, documentation, testing and assessment of changes on other IT components; and implementation protocols.

The change management process also needs to be integrated with other IT processes, including incident management, problem management, availability management and infrastructure change control.

In addition, development and operations (DevOps) and associated software development methodologies (e.g., Agile and Lean) introduce newer risk to the change management process. This means that traditional control test techniques do not fully apply, which results in a need for auditors to adopt automation testing strategies.

2.22 Alignment of PCAOB Standards and COBIT 2019

This section provides high-level guidance on mapping from AS 2201*: An Audit of Internal Control Over Financial Reporting That Is Integrated with An Audit of Financial Statements* to COBIT 2019 to allow management to meet SOX requirements. This mapping is reinforced by more detailed guidance in Appendix A.

2.22.1 Entity-Level Controls

The identification and evaluation of entity-level controls are given considerable weight in AS 2201. **Figure 2.3** lists the COBIT 2019 objectives that map at a high level to AS 2201 entity-level controls. Seventeen COBIT IT governance and management objectives are applicable to entity-level controls. Appendix A provides detailed guidance on the evaluation of the operating effectiveness of these objectives. Given the rather wide-ranging nature of entity-level controls, the guidance in Appendix A is presented as an internal control questionnaire.

In some cases, COBIT 2019 objectives may be relevant to both entity-level and IT general controls. For example, APO13 *Managed Security* and APO10 *Managed Vendors* have features of entity-level and IT general controls.

Figure 2.3—COBIT 2019 Entity-Level Controls Relevant to PCAOB

Entity-level COBIT 2019 Objectives	COBIT 2019 Objective ID
Ensured Governance Framework Setting and Maintenance	EDM01
Ensured Risk Optimization	EDM03
Ensured Stakeholder Engagement	EDM05
Managed I&T Management Framework	APO01
Managed Strategy	APO02
Managed Human Resources	APO07
Managed Vendors	APO10
Managed Quality	APO11
Managed Risk	APO12
Managed Data	APO14
Managed Solutions Identification and Build	BAI03
Managed Projects	BAI11
Managed Operations	DSS01
Managed Performance and Conformance Monitoring	MEA01
Managed System of Internal Control	MEA02

Figure 2.3—COBIT 2019 Entity-Level Controls Relevant to PCAOB *(cont.)*	
Entity-level COBIT 2019 Objectives	**COBIT 2019 Objective ID**
Managed Compliance With External Requirements	MEA03
Managed Assurance	MEA04

2.22.2 IT General Controls

Figure 2.4 shows the high-level alignment of COBIT 2019 objectives that relate to general IT controls with PCAOB AS 2201, formerly AS 5. These controls have a direct impact on the audit of the effectiveness of internal controls over financial reporting, specifically for Sections 302 and 404 of the Sarbanes-Oxley Act. The detailed management practices and activities for these objectives are also provided in Appendix A.

Note

A mapping of COBIT 2019 objectives for SOX to the COSO framework is provided in Chapter 3.

Figure 2.4—Mapping PCAOB AS 2201 IT General Controls and COBIT 2019 Objectives for SOX

COBIT 2019 Objective Related to IT General Controls for SOX	COBIT 2019 Objective ID	PCAOB AS 2201 IT General Controls			
		Program Development	Program Changes	Computer Operations	Access to Programs and Data
Managed Service Agreements	APO09	•	•	•	•
Managed Vendors	APO10	•	•	•	•
Managed Security	APO13			•	•
Managed Requirements Definition	BAI02	•	•		
Managed Solutions Identification and Build	BAI03	•	•		
Managed Availability and Capacity	BAI04	•	•		
Managed IT Changes	BAI06		•	•	•
Managed IT Change Acceptance and Transitioning	BAI07	•	•	•	•
Managed Configuration	BAI10		•	•	•
Managed Operations	DSS01	•		•	•
Managed Service Requests and Incidents	DSS02	•	•	•	
Managed Problems	DSS03			•	
Managed Continuity	DSS04			•	•
Managed Security Services	DSS05			•	•
Managed Business Process Controls	DSS06			•	•

2.22.3 Application Controls

Application controls are a very important consideration for maintaining the viability of ICFR. They are discussed in Chapter 4, and Appendix C provides detailed guidance on application controls.

Page intentionally left blank

Chapter 3
Role of the COSO Framework and Its Relationship to COBIT 2019

3.1 Introduction

SOX legislation and the PCAOB do not mandate a particular control framework.

SOX legislation does, however, require "management to base its evaluation of the effectiveness of the company's ICFR on a suitable, recognized control framework (also known as control criteria) established by a body or group that followed due-process procedures."[52] Although enterprises have flexibility in their choice of an internal control framework, in practice, many enterprises choose to adopt the Internal Control – Integrated Framework promulgated by COSO. The COSO framework definitions of control objectives, entity-level controls and control domains are consistently in use as a guide for enterprises that are required to comply with SOX Sections 302 and 404. However, COSO gives only broad guidance on IT controls. This publication maps COBIT 2019 to COSO, showing how the two frameworks complement each other for purposes of SOX requirements.

COBIT 2019 is a comprehensive framework for the governance and management of enterprise I&T, comprising five domains, 40 governance and management objectives, and over 200 governance and management practices and activities (see Chapter 2). The framework includes controls that address all aspects of I&T governance, but only those significant to financial reporting have been used to develop this publication. COBIT 2019 provides both entity-level and activity-level objectives (called governance and management practices and activities in COBIT 2019) along with associated controls.

3.2 COSO

COSO is a voluntary private-sector organization that is dedicated to the development of guidance in the areas of risk and control, which enable good organizational governance and the reduction of fraud. COSO was formed in 1985 to sponsor the National Commission on Fraudulent Financial Reporting, an independent organization that is often referred to as the Treadway Commission.

The sponsoring organizations of the National Commission on Fraudulent Financial Reporting include the AICPA®, American Accounting Association (AAA), Financial Executives International (FEI), Institute of Internal Auditors (IIA®) and Institute of Management Accountants (IMA®). The following sections provide insight into the COSO framework and its implications for IT. The COSO Internal Control – Integrated Framework establishes five components and 17 principles that ensure that control requirements related to the five key components are met.[53]

The five key component areas are:

- Control environment
- Risk assessment
- Control activities
- Information and communication
- Monitoring activities

[52] *Op cit* US Government Publishing Office, "Public Law 107-204 107th Congress"
[53] *Op cit* COSO, "Internal Control – Integrated Framework, Executive Summary." Used with permission.

COSO Internal Control – Integrated Framework introduces the definition of internal control:

> *...a process, effected by an entity's board of directors, management, and other personnel, designed to provide reasonable assurance regarding the achievement of objectives relating to operations, reporting, and compliance.*
>
> *This definition reflects certain fundamental concepts. Internal control is:*
>
> - *Geared to the achievement of objectives in one or more categories—operations, reporting, and compliance*
> - *A process consisting of ongoing tasks and activities—a means to an end, not an end in itself*
> - *Effected by people—not merely about policy and procedure manuals, systems and forms, but about people and the actions they take at every level of an organization to affect internal control*
> - *Able to provide reasonable assurance—but not absolute assurance, to an entity's senior management and board of directors*
> - *Adaptable to the entity structure—flexible in application for the entire entity or for a particular subsidiary, division, operating unit, or business process*[54]

Internal control has five integrated components, according to COSO:

- **Control environment**—"...the set of standards, processes, and structures that provide the basis for carrying out internal control across the organization."[55]
- **Risk assessment**—Identification and evaluation of relevant risk to enterprise objectives inform decisions regarding risk management.
- **Control activities**—"...actions established through policies and procedures that help ensure that management's directives to mitigate risks to the achievement of objectives are carried out."[56]
- **Information and communication**—"Information is necessary for the entity to carry out internal control responsibilities to support the achievement of its objectives. Management obtains or generates and uses relevant and quality information from both internal and external sources to support the functioning of other components of internal control. Communication is the continual, iterative process of providing, sharing, and obtaining necessary information."[57]
- **Monitoring activities**—"Ongoing evaluations, separate evaluations, or some combination of the two are used to ascertain whether each of the five components of internal control, including controls to effect the principles within each component, is present and functioning."[58]

The COSO framework provides for three categories of objectives, which allow organizations to focus on different aspects of internal control:

- **Operations objectives**—Pertain to effectiveness and efficiency of the entity's operations, including operational and financial performance goals and safeguarding assets against loss[59]
- **Reporting objectives**—Pertain to internal and external financial and nonfinancial reporting and may encompass reliability, timeliness, transparency or other terms as set forth by regulators, recognized standard setters, or entity policies[60]
- **Compliance objectives**—Pertain to adherence to laws and regulations to which the entity is subject[61]

3.3 Relationship of Objectives and Components

A direct relationship exists between objectives, which are what an entity strives to achieve; components, which represent what is required to achieve the objectives; and the organizational structure of the entity (the operating units, legal entities and other). The relationship can be depicted in the form of a cube, as illustrated in **figure 3.1**.

[54] *Ibid.*
[55] *Ibid.*
[56] *Ibid.*
[57] *Ibid.*
[58] *Ibid.*
[59] *Ibid.*
[60] *Ibid.*
[61] *Ibid.*

Figure 3.1 columns represent the three categories of internal control objectives—operations, reporting and compliance. The rows represent the five components of internal control. The entity organizational structure is represented by the third dimension.[62]

Figure 3.1—COSO Framework Objectives, Components and Organizational Structural Model

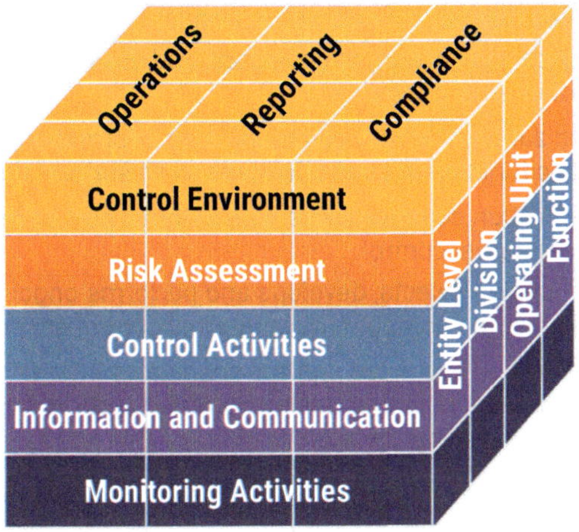

Source: COSO, "Internal Control – Integrated Framework, Executive Summary," USA, May 2013. Used with permission.

Figure 3.2 relates the COSO components to COSO principles.

Figure 3.2—COSO Components and Principles

Components	Principles
Control Environment	1. The organization demonstrates a commitment to integrity and ethical values. 2. The board of directors demonstrates independence from management and exercises oversight of the development and performance of internal control. 3. Management establishes, with board oversight, structures, reporting lines, and appropriate authorities and responsibilities in the pursuit of objectives. 4. The organization demonstrates a commitment to attract, develop and retain competent individuals in alignment with objectives. 5. The organization holds individuals accountable for their internal control responsibilities in the pursuit of objectives.
Risk Assessment	6. The organization specifies objectives with sufficient clarity to enable the identification and assessment of risk relating to objectives. 7. The organization identifies risk to the achievement of its objectives across the entity and analyzes risk as a basis for determining how the risk should be managed. 8. The organization considers the potential for fraud in assessing risk to the achievement of objectives. 9. The organization identifies and assesses changes that could significantly impact the system of internal control.

[62] *Ibid.*

Figure 3.2—COSO Components and Principles *(cont.)*

Components	Principles
Control Activities	10. The organization selects and develops control activities that contribute to the mitigation of risk to ensure the achievement of objectives to acceptable levels.
	11. The organization selects and develops general control activities over technology to support the achievement of objectives.
	12. The organization deploys control activities through policies that establish what is expected and procedures that put policies into action.
Information and Communication	13. The organization obtains, or generates, and uses relevant, quality information to support the functioning of internal control.
	14. The organization internally communicates information, including objectives and responsibilities for internal control, necessary to support the functioning of internal control.
	15. The organization communicates with external parties regarding matters affecting the functioning of internal control.
Monitoring Activities	16. The organization selects, develops and performs ongoing and/or separate evaluations to ascertain whether the components of internal control are present and functioning.
	17. The organization evaluates and communicates internal control deficiencies in a timely manner to those parties responsible for taking corrective action, including senior management and the board of directors, as appropriate.

Source: COSO, "Internal Control – Integrated Framework, Executive Summary," USA, 2013. Used with permission.

3.4 Applying the COSO Framework to IT and COBIT 2019

For SOX compliance efforts, it is important to demonstrate how IT controls support the COSO framework. COSO uses the term technology to refer to all computerized systems, including software applications and operational control systems. However, the COSO framework does not address other specific IT process areas, such as IT service management or information security, and notes the following:

The principles presented in the COSO framework do not change with the introduction of information technology. Information technology affects which specific internal controls are required; however, overall COSO principles remain the same and need to be followed, with or without information technology. Further, the COSO principles are also not affected by changing technologies.[63]

As presented earlier in the chapter, the COSO framework divides internal control into five components. **Figure 3.3** shows that all of the components need to be in place and integrated to achieve the control objectives necessary for effective financial reporting. COBIT 2019 provides similar detailed guidance for IT. The five components of the COSO framework—beginning with identifying the control environment and culminating in the monitoring of internal controls—is the horizontal layer of the three-dimensional cube. The COBIT 2019 control areas, beginning with the governance domain of Evaluate, Direct and Monitor (EDM) through the management domain of Monitor, Evaluate and Assess (MEA), make up the horizontal layer of the cube. They are applicable to all five components of the COSO framework, individually and in aggregate.

[63] *Ibid.*

Figure 3.3—Mapping COBIT to the COSO Cube

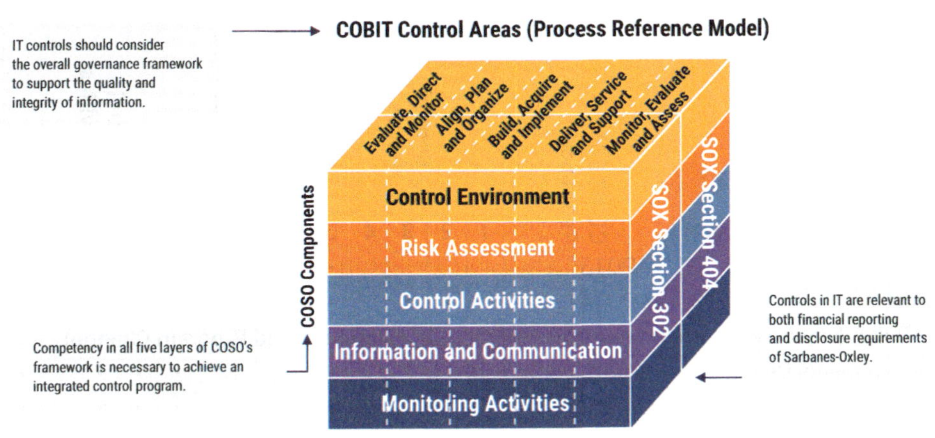

Source: Adapted from COSO, "Internal Control – Integrated Framework, Executive Summary," USA, 2013. Used with permission.

This edition of *IT Control Objectives for Sarbanes-Oxley* provides a list of controls to help ensure that all 17 principles in the COSO Internal Control – Integrated Framework are followed from an IT perspective. **Figure 3.4** shows a high-level summary of the COBIT 2019 objectives that are most relevant for SOX and their alignment to the COSO framework components and principles. Appendix B complements this material with a detailed mapping of specific COBIT 2019 objectives to the 17 COSO Internal Control – Integrated Framework principles.

Figure 3.4—Summary COBIT Areas/COSO Components

Entity Level	Activity Level	Detailed Activity/Objective Level	COBIT 2019 Reference	COSO Component: Control Environment					Risk Assessment				Control Activities			Information and Communication			Monitoring Activities	
				Principles: 1	2	3	4	5	6	7	8	9	10	11	12	13	14	15	16	17
Evaluate, Direct and Monitor (EDM) (IT Environment)																				
•		Ensured Governance Framework Setting and Maintenance	EDM01	•	•	•		•	•	•	•					•	•		•	•
•		Ensured Risk Optimization	EDM03		•		•	•	•	•						•	•		•	•
•		Ensured Stakeholder Engagement	EDM05		•			•								•	•	•	•	•
Align, Plan and Organize (APO) (IT Environment)																				
•	•	Managed I&T Management Framework	APO01	•		•	•	•			•	•			•	•	•			•
•		Managed Strategy	APO02				•	•	•							•	•		•	
•		Managed Human Resources	APO07	•			•				•		•		•	•	•		•	
	•	Managed Service Agreements	APO09					•	•				•	•		•	•	•	•	•
•	•	Managed Vendors	APO10					•	•	•	•	•	•	•		•	•	•	•	•
•		Managed Quality	APO11					•	•						•	•	•		•	•
•		Managed Risk	APO12					•	•	•	•	•				•	•			

Figure 3.4—Summary COBIT Areas/COSO Components *(cont.)*

Entity Level	Activity Level	Detailed Activity/Objective Level	COBIT 2019 Reference	COSO Component: Control Environment					Risk Assessment				Control Activities			Information and Communication			Monitoring Activities	
			Principles	1	2	3	4	5	6	7	8	9	10	11	12	13	14	15	16	17
•	•	Managed Security	APO13					•	•	•	•	•		•		•	•			
•	•	Managed Data	APO14		•	•		•	•	•	•	•		•	•	•	•		•	•
		Build, Acquire and Implement (BAI) (Program Development and Program Change)																		
	•	Managed Requirements Definition	BAI02						•			•	•	•		•	•			
•	•	Managed Solutions Identification and Build	BAI03						•			•	•	•		•	•		•	•
	•	Managed Availability and Capacity	BAI04									•	•	•		•	•		•	•
	•	Managed IT Changes	BAI06						•		•	•	•	•		•	•			
	•	Managed IT Change Acceptance and Transitioning	BAI07						•	•	•	•	•	•		•	•			
	•	Managed Configuration	BAI10						•		•	•	•	•		•	•			
•		Managed Projects	BAI11													•			•	•
		Deliver, Service and Support (DSS) (Operations and Access to Programs and Data)																		
•	•	Managed Operations (including outsourced services)	DSS01						•	•	•	•	•	•	•	•	•			
	•	Managed Service Requests and Incidents	DSS02						•				•	•		•	•		•	•
	•	Managed Problems	DSS03						•				•	•		•	•			
	•	Managed Backup Arrangements	DSS04.07						•				•	•		•	•			
	•	Managed Security Services	DSS05					•	•	•	•		•	•		•	•		•	•
	•	Managed Business Process Controls (including application controls)	DSS06					•	•	•	•		•	•		•	•			
		Monitor, Evaluate and Assess (MEA) (IT Environment)																		
•		Managed Performance and Conformance Monitoring	MEA01					•	•							•	•		•	•
•	•	Managed System of Internal Control	MEA02					•	•	•	•	•	•			•	•		•	•
•		Managed Compliance With External Requirements	MEA03					•			•				•	•	•		•	•
•		Managed Assurance	MEA04	•	•	•	•	•	•	•	•	•	•			•	•		•	•

Source: Adapted from ISACA, *IT Control Objectives for Sarbanes-Oxley: Using COBIT® 5 in the Design and Implementation of Internal Controls Over Financial Reporting, 3rd Edition*, USA, 2014, *https://store.isaca.org/s/store#/store/browse/detail/a2S4w000004Ko9JEAS*

3.5 Control Environment Component

The control environment affects the entire entity. It creates the foundation for effective internal control and sets the tone at the top of the organization. Five COSO principles are related to the control environment, as shown in **figure 3.2**. The control environment primarily addresses the entity level. COSO principle 3 is used in the following example.

Example:

COSO principle 3—"Management establishes, with board oversight, structures, reporting lines, and appropriate authorities and responsibilities in the pursuit of objectives."[64]

Four COBIT 2019 governance and management objectives align to this principle:

- EDM01 *Ensured Governance Framework Setting and Maintenance*
- APO01 *Managed I&T Management Framework*
- APO14 *Managed Data*
- MEA04 *Managed Assurance*

Example COBIT 2019 control objective:

APO01.05 *Establish roles and responsibilities*. Define and communicate roles and responsibilities for enterprise I&T, including authority levels, responsibilities and accountability.

3.6 Risk Assessment Component

Risk assessment involves management identification and analysis of relevant risk to achieving predetermined objectives, which form the basis for determining control activities. A risk assessment is required for both entity-level and the activity-level controls (for a specific process or business unit). Four principles are associated with this component. COSO principle 8 is used in the following example.

Example:

COSO principle 8—"The organization considers the potential for fraud in assessing risks to the achievement of objectives."[65]

Sixteen COBIT 2019 objectives align to this principle:

- EDM01 *Ensured Governance Framework Setting and Maintenance*
- APO01 *Managed I&T Management Framework*
- APO07 *Managed Human Resources*
- APO10 *Managed Vendors*
- APO12 *Managed Risk*
- APO13 *Managed Security*
- APO14 *Managed Data*
- BAI06 *Managed IT Changes*
- BAI07 *Managed IT Change Acceptance and Transitioning*
- BAI10 *Managed Configuration*
- DSS01 *Managed Operations*

[64] *Ibid.*
[65] *Ibid.*

- DSS05 *Managed Security Services*
- DSS06 *Managed Business Process Controls*
- MEA02 *Managed System of Internal Control*
- MEA03 *Managed Compliance With External Requirements*
- MEA04 *Managed Assurance*

Example COBIT 2019 control objectives:

- DSS05.04 *Manage user identity and logical access.* Specifically authenticate all access to information assets based on the individual's role or business rules. Coordinate with business units that manage authentication within applications that are used in business processes to ensure that authentication controls have been properly administered to reduce or prevent fraud.
- DSS06.03 *Manage roles, responsibilities, access privileges and levels of authority.* Allocate access rights and privileges based on the minimum that is required to perform job activities, based on predefined job roles. Remove or revise access rights immediately, if the job role changes or the staff member leaves the business process area. Periodically review to ensure that the access is appropriate for the current threats, risk, technology and business need.

3.7 Control Activities Component

Control activities are the policies, procedures and practices that are in place to ensure achievement of business objectives and risk optimization. Control activities specifically address each control objective to mitigate identified risk.

The IT-related general controls include the following four types of control that are included in the selection of the appropriate SOX-related general controls in the recommended COBIT 2019 governance and management objectives for SOX compliance:

- Data center operation controls—Controls such as job setup and scheduling, operator actions, and data backup and recovery procedures
- System software controls—Controls over the effective acquisition, implementation and maintenance of system software, database management, telecommunications software, security software and utilities
- Access security controls—Controls that prevent inappropriate and unauthorized use of the system across all layers of systems, operating system, database and application
- Application system development and maintenance controls—Controls over development methodology, including system design and implementation that outline specific phases, documentation requirements, change management, approvals and checkpoints to control the development or maintenance of the project

Three COSO principles are aligned to the control activities component. COSO principle 11 (technology controls) is used in the following example. This is one of the key COSO principles for IT, and, as a result, is a major focus for SOX compliance.

Example:

COSO principle 11—"The organization selects and develops general control activities over technology to support the achievement of objectives."[66]

Sixteen COBIT 2019 management objectives align to this principle:

[66] *Ibid.*

- APO09 *Managed Service Agreements*
- APO10 *Managed Vendors*
- APO13 *Managed Security*
- APO14 *Managed Data*
- BAI02 *Managed Requirements Definition*
- BAI03 *Managed Solutions Identification and Build*
- BAI04 *Managed Availability and Capacity*
- BAI06 *Managed IT Changes*
- BAI07 *Managed IT Change Acceptance and Transitioning*
- BAI10 *Managed Configuration*
- DSS01 *Managed Operations*
- DSS02 *Managed Service Requests and Incidents*
- DSS03 *Managed Problems*
- DSS04 *Managed Continuity*
- DSS05 *Managed Security Services*
- DSS06 *Managed Business Process Controls*

Example COBIT 2019 control objectives:

- BAI04.01 *Assess current availability, performance and capacity and create a baseline*. Assess availability, performance and capacity of services and resources to ensure that cost-justifiable capacity and performance are available to support business needs and deliver against service level agreements (SLAs). Create availability, performance and capacity baselines for future comparison.
- DSS04.07 *Manage backup arrangements*. Define requirements for onsite and offsite storage of backup data that meet business requirements. Consider the accessibility required to back up data.

3.8 Information and Communication Component

The COSO framework states that an appropriate flow of information is necessary at all levels of an organization to run the business and achieve the entity control objectives. In COBIT 2019, information is part of the overall focus of the governance and management framework (information and related technology as enterprise assets) and a supporting enabler with associated attributes. Facilitating effective communication, by providing a common language framework for governance of enterprise IT is a key purpose of COBIT 2019.

The IT organization processes most financial reporting information. However, the scope of activities undertaken by the IT organization is usually much broader than the support of financial reporting. IT may also assist in implementing mechanisms such as a move to a cloud solution or implementation of a new executive decision support system.

The COSO framework states that there are certain criteria that affect the quality of information; these should include ascertaining whether the information is:

- **Appropriate**—Is it the right information?
- **Timely**—Is it available when required and reported in the right period of time?
- **Current**—Is it the latest available information?
- **Accurate**—Are the data correct?
- **Accessible**—Can authorized individuals gain access to it as necessary?

Three COSO information and communication principles are aligned to the COBIT information component. COSO principle 15 is used in the following example.

Example:

COSO principle 15—"The organization communicates with external parties regarding matters affecting the functioning of internal control."[67]

Four COBIT 2019 governance and management objectives align to this principle:

- EDM05 *Ensured Stakeholder Engagement*
- APO01 *Managed I&T Management Framework*
- APO09 *Managed Service Agreements*
- APO10 *Managed Vendors*

Example COBIT 2019 control objectives:

- EDM05.02 *Direct stakeholder engagement, communication and reporting.*
- EDM05.03 *Monitor stakeholder engagement* ensures that the communication to stakeholders is effective and timely and that a reliable, consistent basis for reporting is established.

3.9 Monitoring Activities Component

Monitoring covers the oversight of internal control by management through continuous and point-in-time assessment processes. Monitoring is becoming increasingly important to IT management. Two COSO framework principles are aligned to this component. COSO principle 17 is used in the following example.

Example

COSO principle 17—"The organization evaluates and communicates internal control deficiencies in a timely manner to those parties responsible for taking corrective action, including senior management and the board of directors, as appropriate."[68]

Seventeen COBIT 2019 governance and management objectives align to this principle:

- EDM01 *Ensured Governance Framework Setting and Maintenance*
- EDM03 *Ensured Risk Optimization*
- EDM05 *Ensured Stakeholder Engagement*
- APO01 *Managed I&T Management Framework*
- APO09 *Managed Service Agreements*
- APO10 *Managed Vendors*
- APO11 *Managed Quality*
- APO14 *Managed Data*
- BAI03 *Managed Solutions Identification and Build*
- BAI04 *Managed Availability and Capacity*
- BAI11 *Managed Projects*

[67] *Ibid.*
[68] *Ibid.*

- DSS02 *Managed Service Requests and Incidents*
- DSS05 *Managed Security Services*
- MEA01 *Managed Performance and Conformance Monitoring*
- MEA02 *Managed System of Internal Control*
- MEA03 *Managed Compliance With External Requirements*
- MEA04 *Managed Assurance*

An example COBIT 2019 control objective:

- MEA03.03 *Confirm external compliance*. Confirm compliance of policies, principles, standards, procedures and methodologies with legal, regulatory and contractual requirements. Regularly review for recurring patterns of compliance failure and assess lessons learned.

Page intentionally left blank

Chapter 4
Application Controls

4.1 Introduction

Organizations are highly dependent on automated processing of information by many software applications that are the foundation for the preparation of financial statements.

IT used to refer to the organizational department with main responsibility for technology, as opposed to I&T, which encompasses all the information the enterprise generates, processes and uses to achieve its goals, as well as the technology to support that throughout the enterprise.[69]

Every aspect of day-to-day modern business activity is dependent on timely, accurate and reliable information—information that is generated, processed, accumulated, stored and reported on by automated information systems. Customers, suppliers, employees, line management, middle management, the C-suite, board of directors, shareholders, regulators and all other stakeholders make decisions based on this information—information whose accuracy, timeliness and reliability depend heavily on the application systems and information technology governance and control processes that support the production of the information. All stakeholders rely on information produced by automated systems to support decision making.

Application controls refer to controls over the processing of transactions and data within an application and are, therefore, specific to each application. Application controls are built into prepackaged software on which management relies to achieve its control objectives. IT general controls are important to the effective operation of those application controls. The objectives of application controls, which may be manual or automated, are to ensure the accuracy, reliability, confidentiality, integrity and availability of the records/data and the validity of the entries made to the application via manual and programmed processing.

Appendix C provides more detailed examples of automated application controls.

4.2 Application Controls Overview

Application controls are a subset of internal controls that relate to an application system and the information that is managed by that application. Timely, accurate and reliable information is critical to enable informed decision making. The timeliness, accuracy and reliability of the information are dependent on the underlying applications systems that are used to generate, process, store and report the information. Application controls are those controls that achieve the business objectives of timely, accurate and reliable information.

Ineffective or nonexistent controls over applications that support financial accounting and reporting create heightened risk of material misstatements in the financial statements due to errors and fraud. Application controls pertain to the scope of individual business processes or application systems, including data edits, separation of business functions, balancing of processing totals, transaction logging and error reporting. Organizations use application controls that are inherent or embedded (e.g., processing controls that ensure transactions are posted to the correct accounting period) in transactional and support applications, and controls that are configurable (e.g., error or rounding tolerances) to manage the risk of material misstatement due to error or fraud.

[69] This chapter leverages ISACA's *COBIT® 2019 Design Guide: Designing an Information and Technology Governance Solution*, USA, 2018, *https://store.isaca.org/s/store#/store/browse/detail/a2S4w000004Ko9bEAC*, and its companion tool kit, which may be downloaded at *https://www.isaca.org/-/media/files/isacadp/project/isaca/knowledge-and-insights/zips/cobit-2019-design-toolkit_tkt_eng_1218.zip?la=en&hash=0E8BC92071EF5FDF474A979F75A0F78CBC775E54.*

Senior management is responsible for the reliability of the information that the enterprise produces and provides to stakeholders or as part of any legal or compliance requirement. Several parties support senior management in this goal and have roles in designing, implementing, monitoring and maintaining application controls. Responsible parties include operational business management, human resource management, finance, IT management and internal audit. Application controls are designed to mitigate key risk, including fraud risk, and are implemented and operating effectively to provide timely, accurate and reliable information.

Ultimately, under Sarbanes-Oxley Sections 302 and 906, the chief executive officer (CEO) and chief financial officer (CFO) have a legal obligation to provide certifications on a quarterly and annual basis. These certifications confirm, among other things, that the enterprise has designed internal controls over financial reporting and disclosure controls and procedures to provide reasonable assurance regarding the reliability of financial reporting and the preparation of financial statements for external purposes in accordance with generally accepted accounting principles.

This chapter focuses on application controls that are related to all types of systems to meet the requirements of Sarbanes-Oxley compliance. The objective is to provide guidance relative to the design, implementation and execution of control activities related to information systems—no matter what type—because each type provides critical information that supports key decision making.

Examples of common application controls:

- Input controls include logical access controls and data entry/field validations (e.g., validation of entered credit card numbers) or field entries being enforced based on predefined values (e.g., pricing information).
- Processing controls are typically configurable and ensure compliance with business rules and workflow rules, including authorizations (e.g., routing and sign-off of purchase requests). Processing controls also include the enforcement of work steps based on enforcement of segregation of duties that separate individuals for initiating transactions, recording transactions and overseeing assets, and based on predefined status transitions (e.g., open > reviewed > closed).
- Output controls address what is done with the data and should compare output results with the intended result by checking the output against the input.
- Integrity controls monitor data as they are processed and when archived in storage to ensure that they remain consistent and correct.
- Management or audit trail reports include manual or hybrid account reconciliations and automated activity logs that provide a processing history so management can track transactions from their source to their output, forwards or backwards, if necessary. These controls also monitor the effectiveness of other controls and identify errors as close as possible to their sources.

Application controls typically can be tested more efficiently for Sarbanes-Oxley purposes than manual controls. The sample size of the application controls often does not depend on the frequency of the control performance (i.e., application controls are either operating effectively or not). In addition, application controls are typically tested one time, as long as the ITGCs are effective, according to the benchmarking approach suggested by PCAOB AS 2201, Appendix B. Sample sizes for manual controls are tied to the frequency with which the controls are performed (e.g., daily, weekly, monthly, quarterly or annually).

4.3 Business Processes and Automated Solutions

Management of the business unit (i.e., the business process owner) is responsible for defining the appropriate business rules to ensure achievement of the enterprise objectives and the requirements for business processes. Automated tasks and activities are a significant, integral component of most business processes. Business and IT should work together to design the business processes, which cover manual procedures and automated solutions in a properly integrated manner.

IT management is typically responsible for implementing the automated solutions that enable achievement of management business rules and objectives and for providing an environment for the reliable operation of those automated solutions.

Business management has overall responsibility for ensuring the integrity of the entire business process, including the operation of manual and automated controls.

Implemented automated solutions typically take one of the following two forms:

- **Management information systems**—These solutions automate the collection and processing of information that is related to the execution and financial aspects of the enterprise's core activities but are also related to the collection and processing of information about enterprise processes, resources and customers. Common examples include integrated ERP systems that automate the collection and processing of financial information.
- **Process automation systems**—These solutions automate specific activities within a process, such as executive information systems/decision support systems (EIS/DSS) used to support business decision making.

Internal auditors have an opportunity to play a crucial role in safeguarding enterprise assets and ensuring the integrity of the control environment when new or significantly upgraded transactional or support applications are implemented. At that time, it is common for manual and automated controls that were in place in the legacy environment to be reviewed and updated for the new environment. Compounding this task is the likelihood that the organization risk profile may have changed because the new or upgraded applications were necessitated by acquisitions, divestitures, or other organizational and business model changes. The new application introduces new risk because of the need to configure new controls. If the risk cannot be mitigated with automated, configurable controls, then new manual controls may be necessary.

Internal auditors can assist and potentially lead efforts to align new or revised business processes with functional capabilities of new or updated software. Internal auditors are well positioned due to their familiarity with existing business processes, their level of experience with flowcharting and walkthrough techniques, and the ability to lead functional design workshops. Finally, internal auditors have a keen sense of where controls are required. They are also independent from management and can navigate the discussion of the cost/benefit of new or revised controls.

It is the responsibility of the chief audit executive to make sure the internal audit function has sufficient competence, experience and training to adequately address IT risk in the organization and to supervise outside consultants who assist in addressing those tasks. Internal auditors must be aware of relevant risk and activities and able to add value, knowledge and expertise to IT risk management services. Lack of involvement of internal auditors in system development and IT infrastructure activities that manage the risk of the organization applications—for example, making sure inherent and configurable controls are operating effectively prior to the live stage of the application—may lead to a much more costly review after the fact (one that finds weaknesses) and the need to retrofit controls.

4.4 Defining Application Controls

For the purposes of this guide, applications consist of the programmed logic and automated business rules that are used to process information. The terms application and automated solution are used in the generic sense—programmed logic and business rules can exist within specific modules, collections of modules can comprise an application, and a collection of applications and related procedures can comprise a system.

Ensuring that application controls are effective is an important business objective. Application controls that are operating effectively ensure the integrity and reliability of information that is used by management to make key decisions about the business and, increasingly, to meet legal and regulatory compliance requirements, including for management assessment of SOX disclosure controls and ICFR compliance. These concepts may not be well understood by business and IT management, despite being relatively well understood by auditors and compliance specialists. It is important to connect risk assessment concepts with the decisions that management must make regarding the control activities necessary to mitigate risk to the level of the accepted risk tolerance of management.

4.5 Attributes of Application Controls

Application controls may be manual business process controls, automated application controls or a hybrid of the two.

Business process controls are control activities performed without the assistance of applications or automated systems. Examples include supervisory approvals; written authorizations, such as a signature on a check; or manual tasks, such as reconciling purchase orders to goods receipt statements. Manual business process controls are subject to the inherent risk of human error and, as a result, are often considered less reliable than automated controls.

Automated application controls can be programmed and embedded within a software application. Examples include input edit checks that validate order quantities and check digits routines that validate the correctness of bank account numbers. Configurable controls are automated application controls that are based on and, therefore, dependent on the configuration of parameters within the application system. For example, a control in an automated purchasing system that allows orders only up to preconfigured authorization limits is, in turn, dependent on controls over how changes to those configurable authorization limits are initiated and approved.

Most commercial and in-house developed integrated financial accounting and reporting systems are heavily dependent on controls that are designed and implemented by configuring parameter tables to establish business rules and workflows. It is necessary to consider the design of controls over the initial configuration and subsequent changes to them to be a separate element of the control design, implementation and annual SOX testing.

Hybrid controls are a combination of manual and automated activities, all of which must operate for the control to be effective. For example, the customer order fulfillment process might include a control where the shipping manager reviews a report of unshipped orders. For this control to be effective, the automated activity (generation of a complete and accurate unshipped orders report) and the manual activity (review and follow-up by management) are necessary for the control activity to be effective.

Hybrid or automation-dependent controls may be mistaken for manual controls. Because all parts of a hybrid control must be effective, if hybrid or automation-dependent controls are incorrectly identified, there is a significant risk that key elements of the true control are not considered as part of the overall design effectiveness. For example, if the review of the unshipped orders report in the previous example was incorrectly identified as a manual control, there is a risk that the design of controls to ensure the completeness and accuracy of the unshipped orders report may be overlooked.

4.6 Preventive vs. Detective Controls

Application controls are also classified as preventive or detective. Preventive application controls prevent an error from occurring (based on predefined business logic or business rules) and are typically executed at the transaction level before an action is performed or confirmed. An example of a preventive application control is an input validation control where the software performs reasonableness and limit checks on financial values entered. Sequence checks for missing items, range checks, check digits and cross-checks are forms of preventive input validation controls that are typically configurable and embedded in the software.

Detective application controls detect errors based on predefined logic or business rules. These controls usually execute after an action has taken place and often cover a group of transactions. An example is a periodic exception report that is generated by the purchasing application that lists critical changes that have been performed to the supplier master file, e.g., changes to supplier bank account numbers.

Preventive controls are typically more efficient and effective than detective controls, especially in regard to an error that results in significant incremental remediation costs and legal or regulatory consequences. Preventive controls may also be easier to automate than detective controls. Detective controls often depend on manual review activities, which may be weak or nonexistent due to staffing limitations or time constraints. Effective control design should consider a balance of preventive and detective controls that meets risk tolerances but is also cost-effective.

4.7 Automated Testing of Application Controls

Automated monitoring and testing of application controls can mitigate risk and make SOX testing more efficient. Effective application controls help organizations to ensure the integrity, accuracy, confidentiality and completeness of data and systems. It is important for IT auditors to plan and perform audits of application controls on a periodic basis and when new applications are implemented or existing applications are upgraded, to determine whether they are designed appropriately and operating effectively.

Application controls monitoring can be automated via dynamic dashboards that monitor configurations and alert organizations to changes in configurations. Exception reports use a predefined rule to identify emergency changes or unusual changes to user access, e.g., changes that create segregation-of-duties conflicts. Additional reports can provide information about user creation, timely revocation of access for terminations and changes in roles. Continuous monitoring can provide insight into change management activities, including whether changes are adequately tested and approved.

Automated testing of controls can range from the development of automated scripts to performance of controls testing to the implementation of continuous testing of controls that is incorporated in a robotic process automation (RPA) solution. For example, an RPA can include bots (i.e., sets of algorithms) that log in and download all the changes on a system during a period and then reconcile them with approvals. An exception report is created for changes that have no approvals or whose approvals were obtained after the changes were live.

4.8 Application Control Risk in a Cloud Environment

There are shared responsibilities between the enterprise and cloud service providers (CSPs) for financial accounting data, cybersecurity, ICFR, SOC reporting and audits. According to AS 2110: *Identifying and Assessing Risks of Material Misstatement* and AS 2201: *An Audit of Internal Control Over Financial Reporting That Is Integrated with An Audit of Financial Statements*, auditors and the internal auditors that support management assessment of ICFR must gain an understanding of the enterprise's control environment and risk to assess the risk of material misstatement of the financial statements.

A good first step is to produce an inventory of audit client cloud activities, including the nature and extent of all CSP vendors and any material changes in such contracts during the audit period under review. If good documentation does not exist, the risk of material misstatement is likely higher and additional audit procedures performed by professionals with specialized cloud audit skills may be required. That means higher external audit fees.[70]

The move to cloud environments, whether a private cloud, public cloud, hybrid cloud or community cloud is a boon to flexibility for how and where the business operates. However, regardless of the approach to cloud adoption, whether via IaaS, SaaS, PaaS, or pay-as-you-go models for infrastructure and applications, new risk is introduced, especially regarding cybersecurity. Moving from on-premises managed hardware and software to a cloud environment necessitates a shift in perspective regarding controls, especially over core application security and user and data security. For example, non-IT employees can develop applications and may have the authority to contract

[70] For more about the impact of cloud environments on external audit firms and their work, see Stein, M.; V. Campitelli; S. Mezzio; "Managing the Impact of Cloud Computing, Perspectives on Vulnerabilities, ERM, and Audit Services," *The CPA Journal*, July 2020, *www.cpajournal.com/2020/07/13/managing-the-impact-of-cloud-computing/*.

directly with CSPs outside the centralized IT procurement process. The risk is anywhere and everywhere—not just in IT. As a result, attention should be given to how remote work enabled by cloud computing affects ICFR and whether the auditors have included new controls in their assessment or evaluated changes to existing controls.

4.8.1 COVID-19 Impact

In 2019 and continuing throughout the 2020 pandemic period, the PCAOB began engaging directly and more often with audit committees. In 2019, the PCAOB reached out to nearly 400 audit committee chairs of US issuers whose audits the regulator inspected. Addressing the risk related to the gradual, then sudden, transition to remote work was the issue that came up most often in those discussions.[71, 72] During its 2020 audit engagement inspections period, the PCAOB asked audit committee chairs how they addressed the impact of COVID-19 on financial reporting and the audit as they performed their oversight duties.

Although audit committee chairs assured the PCAOB that the impact on ICFR was managed, maintained or adjusted as necessary, many also identified cyber-related risk—such as increased phishing attempts and email security—as being a major issue with the move to remote work. Audit committee chairs were pressing the auditors on testing the effectiveness of cyber-related controls that are in the scope of the audit. Having data already stored in the cloud eased the transition to remote work but presented new risk on which audit committees and auditors were required to focus. Attention should be given to how remote work enabled by cloud computing affects ICFR and whether the auditors included new controls in the assessment or evaluated changes to existing ones. For example, remote work strains the ability to maintain proper segregation of duties.

4.9 Application Controls in a Cloud Environment

Organizations must ensure that the control postures of third parties providing IaaS, SaaS, PaaS cloud services are evaluated. This is particularly critical where outsourced applications supply material balances to the financial statements. The focus of the evaluation should include, but not be limited to, change control, security and identity and access management. In addition, having a solid asset inventory will help ensure no critical applications or underlying infrastructure are excluded from the analysis.

4.9.1 Security Controls in Cloud Applications

Cloud applications such as Google Drive™, Box® and Dropbox® provide services to many customers. Cybercriminals can exploit security vulnerabilities that exist in cloud apps such as these to create large-scale attacks. Design flaws occur because of development choices that have not gone through appropriate security reviews before design and development. As a result, cloud applications may be vulnerable to poor single sign-on (SSO) implementations, insecure authentication mechanisms and other security-deficient design decisions.

The CSA Egregious Eleven threats resulting from cloud computing include metastructure and applistructure failures.[73] The CSA report states that the most frequent examples of meta/applistructure failures for cloud application customers relate to identity and access management issues. Many organizations have not implemented more robust security capabilities than usernames and passwords. This occurs despite SSO, identity federation and multi-factor authentication (MFA) being offered—and easily implemented—within most cloud applications.

[71] PCAOB, "Audit Committee Resource: 2021 Inspections Outlook," April 2021, *https://pcaob-assets.azureedge.net/pcaob-dev/docs/default-source/documents/audit-committee-resource-2021-inspections-outlook.pdf?sfvrsn=81720da4_6*

[72] PCAOB, "Conversations with Audit Committee Chairs: COVID-19 and the Audit," *https://pcaobus.org/Documents/Conversations-with-Audit-Committee-Chairs-Covid.pdf*

[73] *Op cit* CSA, "Top Threats to Cloud Computing: The Egregious 11"

Even the largest audit firms are vulnerable if they perpetuate poor practices internally while promoting best practices to clients. In 2017, Deloitte® acknowledged a breach of its internal email systems that had reportedly been going on since 2016.[74] The breach involved the compromise of all administrator accounts at the firm and the entire Deloitte internal Microsoft Office 365® email system, after Deloitte relied on a single password for its administrator account.

During that same year, a massive breach at big-three consumer credit bureau Equifax® involved several months of unauthorized access in which intruders stole Social Security numbers, birth dates and addresses of 143 million Americans. The consumer information that Equifax sells to banks and other organizations generates most of its revenues, but Equifax auditor Ernst & Young® did not spot the vulnerability that led to the hack.[75] The Equifax intruders gained access to such a large amount of sensitive consumer data via a vulnerability in the Equifax website, which might suggest that Equifax fell behind in applying security-related patches or updates to its Internet-facing web applications.

Access controls limit exposure of enterprise data to the Internet by limiting who has access to the cloud services. Amazon® and other cloud providers consistently provide warnings to customers to avoid allowing storage drive contents to be accessible to anyone with an Internet connection. Data stored on the cloud should also always be encrypted to limit damage if unauthorized access does occur.

Multi-factor authentication is a control that provides an extra layer of protection on top of basic access controls, such as username and password. MFA should be enabled to restrict access to management consoles, dashboards and privileged accounts. IaaS keys, such as Amazon Web Services (AWS)™ keys, should also be secured and not shared in source code repositories or on public forums.

Customers of cloud service providers should always turn on security logging and monitoring, and then provide sufficient staff to review reports that flag unauthorized access attempts and similar issues.

Finally, when sharing applications and data externally, policies to block and protect downloads to unknown devices and monitor low-trust sessions act as additional controls to prevent unauthorized access and data leakage.

4.9.2 Additional Controls for Cloud Applications

Understanding the responsibility boundaries between an IaaS provider, such as Amazon, Microsoft® and Google®, and their customers is critically important. IaaS providers administer security for their own physical data centers and the server hardware that runs the virtual machines. Their customers are responsible for protecting their own virtual machines and applications. Cloud providers may offer services and tools to implement secure customer workloads, but the customer administrator is still required to implement those tools. If customers do not install tools that protect and maintain their own networks, users and applications, it is not going to matter what the IaaS providers do.

Multicloud environments become complicated to administer, manage and control. When a complex environment is combined with poor inventory and administration of all the cloud services in use at an enterprise, the risk of a misconfiguration issue that can lead to data loss or a breach increases.

The CSA Cloud Controls Matrix (CCM)™ is specifically designed to provide fundamental security principles to guide cloud vendors and to assist prospective cloud customers in assessing the overall security risk of a cloud provider.[76] The foundations rest on its customized relationship to other industry-accepted security standards, regulations and controls frameworks, such as International Organization for Standardization (ISO)/International

[74] Krebs, B.; "Source: Deloitte Breach Affected All Company Email, Admin Accounts," Krebs on Security, 25 September 2017, *https://krebsonsecurity.com/2017/09/source-deloitte-breach-affected-all-company-email-admin-accounts/*

[75] McKenna, F.; "Equifax auditors are on the hook for data security risk controls," MarketWatch, 2 October 2017, *www.marketwatch.com/story/equifax-auditors-are-on-the-hook-for-data-security-risk-controls-2017-10-02*

[76] CSA, Cloud Controls Matrix (CCM), Version 4, *https://cloudsecurityalliance.org/research/cloud-controls-matrix/*

Electrotechnical Commission (IEC) 27001/27002, ISACA's COBIT, PCI DSS, NIST, Jericho Forum™ and North American Electric Reliability Corporation™ Critical Infrastructure Protection (NERC CIP).

Controls that prevent data loss include tools and processes that ensure that sensitive data, including client information, are not lost, misused or accessed by unauthorized users. An enterprise data loss prevention solution can monitor and block access to personal email, cloud-based file sharing services, social media sites and removable media, such as USBs and CDs, if a threat is perceived.[77] A vulnerability management program implements controls, such as routine scans of software code, web applications, servers and databases, workstations, and endpoints within the organization and applicable third-party providers. Perimeter security controls manage, monitor and inspect all incoming and outgoing network traffic to prevent unauthorized or harmful traffic. These controls include firewalls, intrusion detection systems, email security capabilities and web proxy systems with content filtering.

Customers can require public cloud vendors to provide ISO 27001 certifications and SOC audit reports that document controls and their effectiveness for use by internal and external auditors. This documentation should be obtained before deciding about a cloud infrastructure or application vendor and periodically afterward to assess changes in their environment as they relate to the enterprise's control environment.

In February 2020, the SEC Office of Compliance Inspections and Examinations (OCIE) issued examination observations related to cybersecurity and operational resiliency practices implemented by a variety of market participants.[78] In the cloud environment, robust vendor management practices are a key control to mitigate risk. OCIE observed that a vendor management program that ensures that vendors meet security requirements and implement appropriate safeguards is imperative. Ensuring that there are procedures for terminating or replacing vendors, including cloud-based service providers, is also important. Enterprises and their internal auditors should ensure that management is leveraging questionnaires based on reviews of industry standards (e.g., SOC 2, Statements on Standards for Attestation Engagements [SSAE] 18) and independent audits of vendors and applications.

A recent poll[79] indicates that 80 percent of US companies need to stay compliant with the EU GDPR. GDPR is a data protection regulation that requires organizations to protect the personal data of the users and the privacy of EU citizens. GDPR data protection requirements include, but are not limited to, providing timely notifications of security incidents; sharing data with the end users if requested, including the right to be forgotten; implementing robust security solutions to monitor the data flow; and preventing security incidents.[80]

Using SOC reports to assess application controls, cybersecurity controls and other ITGC for outsourced operations and infrastructure are discussed in more detail in Chapter 5.

4.10 Application Control Objectives

The goal of application controls is to provide reasonable assurance of the achievement of management objectives relative to a given application. Management objectives are typically articulated through the definition of specific functional requirements for the application, the definition of business rules for processing information through the application and the definition of manual procedures that support the objectives of the automated processes.

[77] US Securities and Exchange Commission, "Cybersecurity and Resiliency Observations," Office of Compliance and Inspections Examinations, 27 January 2020, *www.sec.gov/files/OCIE%20Cybersecurity%20and%20Resiliency%20Observations.pdf*

[78] US Securities and Exchange Commission, "2020 Examination Priorities," Office of Compliance and Inspections Examinations, *www.sec.gov/about/offices/ocie/national-examination-program-priorities-2020.pdf*

[79] Ashford, W.; "GDPR Fines May Affect Almost 80% of US Firms, Poll Shows," Computer Weekly, 8 November 2017, *www.computerweekly.com/news/450429701/GDPR-fines-may-affect-almost-80-of-US-firms-poll-shows*

[80] Sood, A.K.; R. Jalil; "Cloudifying Threats—Understanding Cloud App Attacks and Defenses," *ISACA® Journal*, 1 January 2018, *https://www.isaca.org/resources/isaca-journal/issues/2018/volume-1/cloudifying-threatsunderstanding-cloud-app-attacks-and-defenses*

Examples of application control objectives follow:

- **Completeness**—The application processes all appropriate transactions, and the resulting information is complete.
- **Accuracy**—All transactions are processed accurately and as intended, and the resulting information is accurate.
- **Validity**—Only valid transactions are processed and the resulting information is valid.
- **Authorization**—Only appropriately authorized transactions have been processed.
- **Segregation of duties**—The application provides for and supports appropriate segregation of duties and responsibilities as defined by management that will prevent or detect fraud.

Appendix B describes the requirements for benchmarking automated controls, which includes establishing and documenting an application baseline. The application control baseline identifies the key application controls, programmed functions and reports that are relied on to ensure complete, accurate, timely and authorized processing and reporting of transactions. Depending on the circumstances, the baseline of the operation of an automated application control needs to be reestablished. Appendix B provides guidelines regarding when to reestablish a baseline. Following are some factors to consider:

- Effectiveness of the IT control environment, including controls over application and system software acquisition and maintenance, access controls and computer operations
- Auditor's understanding of the nature of changes, if any, on the specific programs that contain the controls
- Nature and timing of other related tests
- Consequences of errors associated with the application control that was benchmarked
- Sensitivity of the control to other business factors that may have changed
- Design attributes of the control

To determine design attributes of the control and whether the controls are relevant to audit, following are some questions that can help:

- Why is the control performed?
- Who performs the control?
- When is it performed?
- How does the control operate?
- Is the control performed with the correct level of precision and sensitivity?
- Is the control impacted by other aspects of internal control?

The information item component for a governance system of I&T is equivalent to the process work products, as described in *COBIT® 2019 Framework: Governance and Management Objectives*. Although no generally accepted or formal method exists for assessing information items, they can be less formally assessed, according to the information reference model that was first presented in *COBIT® 5: Enabling Information*.[81]

To satisfy business objectives, information needs to satisfy certain criteria that COBIT 2019 refers to as the business requirements for information and contains certain information requirements and enabler goals:

- Appropriateness
- Relevance
- Understandability
- Interpretability
- Objectivity

[81] ISACA, *COBIT® 5: Enabling Information*, USA, 2012, *https://store.isaca.org/s/store#/store/browse/detail/a2S4w000004KoCHEA0*

The efficiency of information refers to the process of obtaining and using information, which takes into consideration the following information goals:

- Believability (Is the information credible and reliable?)
- Availability (Is the information accessible and secure?)
- Integrity
- Accuracy (Is the information free from error?) and complete
- Confidentiality (Is restrictive access in place?)
- Reputable

These information criteria can vary, depending on the nature of the specific business process. Accomplishment of these information criteria comes from a system of internal control activities. Some of these control activities (application controls) are employed within the business processes and application systems themselves, while others (ITGCs) may be employed within the IT processes and services that manage the environment within which the applications operate.

COBIT 2019 provides a specific management control process—DSS06 *Managed Business Process Controls*, which is provided with the control processes outlined for ITGCs. This process includes the provision of control objectives for application controls. DSS06 provides a link between ITGCs and application controls. **Figure 4.1** summarizes six application control areas in DSS06.

Figure 4.1—DSS06 Application Control Areas

COBIT 2019 Reference	Management Practices (Control Objectives)	Management Practice Description (Control Activities Summary)
DSS06.01	Align control activities embedded in business processes with enterprise objectives.	Continually assess and monitor the execution of business process activities and related controls (based on enterprise risk), to ensure that processing controls align with business needs.
DSS06.02	Control the processing of information.	Operate the execution of the business process activities and related controls, based on enterprise risk. Ensure that information processing is valid, complete, accurate, timely and secure (i.e., reflects legitimate and authorized business use).
DSS06.03	Manage roles, responsibilities, access privileges and levels of authority.	Manage business roles, responsibilities, levels of authority and segregation of duties needed to support the business process objectives. Authorize access to all information assets related to business information processes, including those under the custody of the business, IT and third parties. This ensures that the business knows where the data are and who is handling data on its behalf.
DSS06.04	Manage errors and exceptions.	Manage business process exceptions and errors and facilitate remediation, executing defined corrective actions and escalating as necessary. This treatment of exceptions and errors provides assurance of the accuracy and integrity of the business information process.
DSS06.05	Ensure traceability and accountability for information events.	Ensure that business information can be traced to an originating business event and associated with accountable parties. This discoverability provides assurance that business information is reliable and has been processed in accordance with defined objectives.
DSS06.06	Secure information assets.	Secure information assets accessible by the business through approved methods, including information in electronic form (e.g., portable media devices, user applications and storage devices, or other methods that create new assets in any form), information in physical form (e.g., source documents or output reports) and information during transit. This benefits the business by providing end-to-end safeguarding of information.

Chapter 5
Using Service Organization Reports for ICFR

5.1 Introduction

Third-party service organizations often play a significant role in an enterprise information technology infrastructure and, therefore, in its ITGCs and application controls environment. Depending on their nature and extent, the outsourced services provided by third-party service organizations may be within the scope of the management assessment of ICFR.

Management should consider the services provided by service organizations in making its assessment of ICFR, in the context of SOX compliance. Management must consider a range of issues when making this assessment. Similarly, internal and external auditors of those organizations must consider the extent and materiality of the services provided by service organizations when designing audit procedures on the functioning of IT controls.

5.2 Assurance for the Operation of Services Organizations

Enterprises in almost every industry contract with third-party service organizations to perform noncore activities efficiently and cost-effectively. These third-party vendors may have the resources, experience and technology infrastructure to accomplish these tasks or complete certain functions better than the enterprises. Services that are commonly outsourced include cloud computing, managed security, health care claims management and processing, customer service, human resources and employee benefits, and sales force automation. However, enterprise management remains accountable for controls over these activities despite delegating these tasks or functions to a service organization. Enterprise management is ultimately accountable to the board of directors, customers, shareholders, regulators and others for the accurate, timely and authorized processing of enterprise data.

Third-party service organizations must have effective and transparent information technology controls over internal and outsourced functions. These vendors must be able to prove to their customers—the organizations that outsource key activities or functions to the service organizations—that controls are in place, operating effectively and can be relied on. Service organizations may be inundated with multiple requests from customers to complete questionnaires and provide responses to audit requests and other *ad hoc* inquiries from customers. Their customers, external auditors and internal auditors are verifying that data are being handled with the same level of control as if the data were being processed directly by the enterprise.

AS 2201: *An Audit of Internal Control Over Financial Reporting That Is Integrated with An Audit of Financial Statements* requires the user organization external auditor to test those entity-level controls that are important to the auditor's conclusion about whether the enterprise has effective internal control over financial reporting. The external auditor's evaluation of entity-level controls can result in increasing or decreasing the testing that the auditor otherwise would have performed on other controls. Entity-level controls include centralized processing and controls including in shared service environments.

During the planning of the audit, the external auditor must gain an understanding of the extent of services provided by service organizations that are part of the user organization information system. The auditor must also evaluate the service organization's controls over those services. That information may be obtained from user manuals, system overviews, technical manuals, the contract between the user organization and the service organization, and reports by service auditors, internal auditors or regulatory authorities.

If the external auditors are unable to obtain sufficient information to plan the audit, they may contact the service organization or request that a service organization auditor be engaged to perform procedures that will supply the necessary information. The external auditors can also visit the service organization and perform the procedures directly. If the external auditors are unable to obtain sufficient evidence to achieve their audit objectives, the user auditors should qualify their opinion or disclaim an opinion on the financial statements because of a scope limitation.

AS 2601: *Consideration of an Entity's Use of a Service Organization* applies to the audit of financial statements of an enterprise that obtains services from another organization that are part of the enterprise information system.[82] When services of a service organization are part of an enterprise information system, AS 2601, paragraph .03 explains that they are considered part of the information and communication component of the enterprise internal control over financial reporting.[83] Therefore, the external auditors consider the activities of the service organization when deciding how much evidence is required to support their opinion.

AS 2601, paragraphs .07 through .16 describe the procedures that the user organization external auditor performs with respect to the activities performed by the service organization:[84]

- Obtain an understanding of the nature of the services provided and the service organization controls over those services that are relevant to the entity internal control and the controls at the user organization over the activities of the service organization.
- Obtain evidence that the controls that are relevant to the auditor's opinion are operating effectively.

AS 2601, paragraph .12 describes the procedure to obtain evidence that the controls at the service organization that are relevant to the external auditor's opinion are operating effectively.[85] Those procedures start with obtaining the service organization auditor's report on controls placed in operation and tests of operating effectiveness, or a report on the application of agreed-on procedures that describes relevant tests of controls. This service auditor's report has the service organization auditor's opinion on the service organization's description of the design of its controls, the tests of controls, and results of those tests performed by the service auditor. The report also includes the service organization auditor's opinion on whether the controls tested were operating effectively during the specified period.

5.3 Reporting of Controls of Service Organizations

Several assurance approaches are available to third-party service organizations to support their responses to user organization requests for reports to support external auditors' opinions on ICFR and other controls. The AICPA® has developed three classes of assurance services for third-party service organizations that are intended for different users and cover different levels of assurance. The reports are prepared in accordance with attestation standard AT-C section 320, *Reporting on an Examination of Controls at a Service Organization Relevant to User Entities' Internal Control Over Financial Reporting* and SSAE 18.

The AICPA System and Organization Controls (SOC) reports are service offerings that CPAs may provide with the evaluation of system-level controls of a service organization or entity-level controls of other organizations.[86] Service organizations conduct a SOC audit because user organizations and their respective external auditors demand them.

5.3.1 SOC 1 Report

The SOC 1® report was previously referred to as SAS70 or SSAE 16, but, as of May 1, 2017, it is covered under the SSAE 18 guidance. SOC 1® – SOC for Service Organizations: ICFR – Report on Controls at a Service Organization Relevant to User Entities' Internal Control over Financial Reporting refers two types of AICPA-sponsored reports that meet the external auditors' ICFR requirements:

[82] PCAOB, AS 2601: *Consideration of an Entity's Use of a Service Organization, https://pcaobus.org/oversight/standards/auditing-standards/details/AS2601*
[83] *Ibid.*
[84] *Ibid.*
[85] *Ibid.*
[86] AICPA, "SOC for Service Organizations: Information for Users and User Entities," *www.aicpa.org/interestareas/frc/assuranceadvisoryservices/users.html*

- A SOC 1 Type 2 report attests to the fairness of the presentation of the management description of the service organization system and the suitability of the design and operating effectiveness of the controls to achieve the related control objectives included in the description throughout a specified period.
- A SOC 1 Type 1 report attests to the fairness of the presentation of the management description of the service organization system and the suitability of the design of the controls to achieve the related control objectives included in the description as of a specified date.

5.3.2 SOC 2 Report

SOC 2® – SOC for Service Organizations: Trust Services Criteria – Report on Controls at a Service Organization Relevant to Security, Availability, Processing Integrity, Confidentiality or Privacy is intended to meet the needs of a broad range of users that need detailed information and assurance about the controls at a service organization relevant to security, availability and processing integrity of the systems that the service organization uses to process users' data.[87] The reports also cover the confidentiality and privacy of the information processed by these systems. These reports can play an important role in overall oversight of a third-party service organization, including compliance with vendor contract requirements.

Rather than ICFR, SOC 2® reports focus on service organization controls that are relevant to AICPA trust service principles (TSPs).[88] Examples of trust service principles are:

- *Security—The system is protected against unauthorized access (both physical and logical). The security TSP is often referred to as the Common Criteria.*
- *Privacy—Personal information is collected, used, retained, disclosed, and destroyed in conformity with the commitments in the entity's privacy notice.*

SOC 2 examinations are specifically designed to address controls at a service organization relevant to the systems used to process users' data. The related report provides users with information needed to understand the effectiveness of controls at the service organization and how those controls integrate with controls at the user entity. To produce a SOC 2 report, service organization management engages the CPA to examine and report on system controls that are relevant to security, availability, processing integrity, confidentiality or privacy as set forth in the AICPA trust services criteria. SOC 2 provides needed transparency into how the risk is assessed and managed. The SOC 2 attestation standard standardizes reporting on the controls at third-party service providers that manage the risk.

Regulators have increased scrutiny around vendor management in the 10 years since SOC 2 was introduced, because organizations are creating complex business arrangements and sharing more data, especially in the cloud. The EU GDPR and the California Consumer Privacy Act (CCPA) have forced many organizations that have customers and other business relationships in both jurisdictions to enhance their data privacy programs. Enhanced SOC 2 reports, also called SOC 2®+ reports, can be used to demonstrate compliance with a wide range of regulatory and industry frameworks, such as those from NIST and ISO.

5.3.3 SOC 3 Report

SOC 3® – SOC for Service Organizations: Trust Services Criteria for General Use Report is similar to a SOC 2 engagement. However, in a SOC 3® examination the practitioner reports on whether controls within the system were effective to provide reasonable assurance that the service commitments and system requirements of the service organization were achieved based on the applicable trust services criteria.[89]

[87] AICPA, "SOC 2® – SOC for Service Organizations: Trust Services Criteria," *https://us.aicpa.org/interestareas/frc/assuranceadvisoryservices/aicpasoc2report.html*

[88] Deloitte, "Achieving third-party reporting proficiency with SOC 2+," *www2.deloitte.com/content/dam/Deloitte/us/Documents/finance/us-advisory-competitive-edge-achieving-third-party.pdf*

[89] AICPA, "SOC 3® – SOC for Service Organizations: Trust Services Criteria for General Use Report," *https://us.aicpa.org/interestareas/frc/assuranceadvisoryservices/aicpasoc3report.html*

Although the requirements and guidance for performing a SOC 3 examination are similar to a SOC 2 examination, the reporting requirements are different. Because of the different reporting requirements, a SOC 2 report is appropriate only for specified parties with sufficient knowledge and understanding of the service organization and the system, whereas a SOC 3 report is ordinarily appropriate for general use. These reports are designed to meet the needs of users who need assurance about the controls at a service organization relevant to security, availability, processing integrity, confidentiality or privacy, but do not have the need for or the knowledge necessary to make effective use of a SOC 2 report. Because they are general-use reports, SOC 3 reports can be freely distributed.

International Standard on Assurance Engagements (ISAE) No. 3402, Assurance Reports on Controls at a Service Organization, was issued in December 2009 by the International Auditing and Assurance Standards Board (IAASB), part of the International Federation of Accountants (IFAC). This standard, comparable to SSAE 18, is intended to provide an international option for public accountants who wish to issue a report for use by user organizations and their auditors (user auditors) on the controls at a service organization that are likely to impact or be a part of the user organization system of internal control over financial reporting. The standard complements International Standard on Auditing (ISA) 402, Audit Considerations Relating to an Entity Using a Service Organization, because reports prepared in accordance with ISAE No. 3402 can provide appropriate evidence under ISA 402.

5.4 Scope of the Report

AS 2201, paragraph .B21 states that the external auditor may require a report that covers a period of time or is as of a specific date. The report obtained from the service provider is then evaluated to determine whether it provides sufficient evidence to support the auditor's opinion. The auditor assesses the following factors when evaluating whether the report provides sufficient evidence:

- The time period covered by the tests of controls and its relation to the as-of date of the management assessment[90]
- The scope of the examination and applications covered, the controls tested, and the way in which tested controls relate to the enterprise controls[91]
- The results of those tests of controls and the service auditor's opinion on the operating effectiveness of the controls[92]

Several issues may result in the scope of a SOC 1 report not being sufficient to provide the evidence that the service organization controls are operating effectively. These issues include the following:

- The description of controls is not relevant or is relevant to only a portion of the outsourced services that are part of the information system.
- The description of controls does not sufficiently cover the service organization locations that provide services to the user enterprise.
- The service organization relies on another organization, (a subservice organization) that has been carved out of the scope of the SSAE 18 report, and accordingly no SSAE 18 report is available from the subservice organization.

SSAE 18 added a set of requirements, including a Complementary Subservice Organization Controls section and the performance of a detailed risk assessment based on the control objectives defined in the report.

The SOC report does not cover monitoring controls over the services provided by the subservice organization(s).

[90] PCAOB, AS 2201: *An Audit of Internal Control Over Financial Reporting That Is Integrated with An Audit of Financial Statements*, PCAOB Release No. 2007-005A, *https://pcaobus.org/oversight/standards/auditing-standards/details/AS2201*

[91] *Ibid.*

[92] *Ibid.*

In these instances, management and the auditor(s) should obtain an understanding of the controls that are placed in operation at the service organization that are not covered by an SSAE 18 report and are relevant to the user enterprise financial statement assertions or obtain evidence that the controls are operating effectively through direct testing or other means.

5.5 Description of System and Its Controls

AS 2201 describes the procedures that the external auditor should perform to assess the controls in place for the service provider system and its activities performed by a service organization. The external auditor's procedures should include:

> *Obtaining an understanding of the controls at the service organization that are relevant to the entity's internal control and the controls at the user organization over the activities of the service organization, and*
> *Obtaining evidence that the controls that are relevant to the auditor's opinion are operating effectively.*[93]

The service organization is responsible for fair presentation of the description of the system and its controls. The service organization external auditor provides an opinion on the fairness of the description, unique aspects of the user enterprise process and financial statement assertions, which may result in the description of the system and its controls not meeting the needs of the user enterprise and its internal and external auditors. Some examples of issues that can arise follow:

- Issue: The description of controls in place at the service organization does not contain a description of the controls that should be in place at the user enterprise. The design of service organization controls usually requires user enterprises to implement certain controls. If the description of service organization controls does not identify such user enterprise controls, the user enterprises and their auditors must consider whether any controls should have been identified. In making this evaluation, user enterprises may wish to compare the sources of potential misstatements that they have identified to the controls from the SSAE 18 report.
- Issue: The description of controls is not presented at a level of detail that is sufficient to permit management or the auditor to:
  - Identify types of user enterprise financial statement assertions that are likely to be affected by the controls and sources of potential misstatements.
  - Consider factors that affect the risk of material misstatement.
  - Support the service organization management assessment with regard to internal control.
  - Support the service auditor's opinion on internal controls.
- Issue: The control objectives that are specified by the management of the service organization do not address all the financial statement risk factors that are identified by user management or do not provide sufficient evidence of the coverage of appropriate risk.
- Issue: The controls that are specified by management of the service organization are not, in the judgment of user management or the auditor(s), sufficient to achieve the specified control objectives as they relate to the user enterprise financial statement assertions.
- Issue: The description of controls does not present sufficient information about the relevant entity-level IT controls to permit user enterprise management or the user auditor(s) to assess their operating effectiveness in establishing, enhancing, or mitigating the effectiveness of the activity-level IT controls.

Enterprise management can address these issues by augmenting the description of controls that are presented in the SSAE 18 report with information available from other sources. This information may need to be supplemented with information obtained directly from the service organization through verbal or written inquiry.

[93] *Op cit* PCAOB, AS 2201: *An Audit of Internal Control Over Financial Reporting That Is Integrated with An Audit of Financial Statements*

5.6 Timing

An inherent trade-off exists between the need for user management and internal and external auditors to have the most current evaluation of service organization controls possible and timely receipt of the SSAE 18 report, such that any control exceptions or control objective qualifications can be assessed and the risk mitigated as needed. This trade-off often means the SSAE 18 report is dated prior to the balance sheet date of the user enterprise. This advance work results in two issues that may need to be addressed.

First, significant changes may have occurred in the controls over the services provided from the period covered by the tests of operating effectiveness to the date of the management assessment. Normally, the user organization's external auditor seeks a comfort letter from the service organization external auditor. If a significant period of time has elapsed between the time period covered by the tests of controls in the service auditor's report and the date specified in the management assessment, additional procedures may have to be performed by the external auditor, including visiting the service organization and performing such procedures directly.

If significant changes have occurred in the controls at the service organization, management and the auditor(s) should consider the following:

- Obtaining an understanding of the controls that have changed and that are relevant to the user enterprise's financial statement assertions
- Obtaining evidence that the controls that have changed are operating effectively. Change notifications, technical manual updates, training materials and other communications from the service organization are often sufficient to permit management and the auditor(s) to understand the effect of the change on the user enterprise financial statement assertions.

However, additional inquiry of service organization personnel, supplemented with the receipt of additional documentation, may be necessary. Evidence that the controls that have changed are operating effectively may be more difficult to obtain. If the service organization maintains effective ITGCs, management and the auditor(s) may be able to evidence the functioning of application control changes at the user enterprise site through direct tests of the application controls or participation in user acceptance testing and inspection of the results of the testing.

In other instances, the controls that have changed may be redundant with controls in place and functioning at the user enterprise. In these instances, management and the auditors may choose to test these redundant controls. Finally, management or the auditor may determine that the control can be tested only at the service organization location.

5.7 Nature and Extent of Testing

When the nature or extent of testing that is performed by the service external auditor is not sufficient to support the service organization's management assessment of controls as they relate to the financial statement assertions, user enterprise management or the auditor need to perform additional procedures. Following are typical issues regarding insufficient test evidence:

- Issue: The tests of operating effectiveness of controls that are specified by the service organization do not provide sufficient evidence to support a conclusion about control risk for the financial statement assertions of the user enterprise. A similar problem exists if there is insufficient testing of controls to address the financial statement risk factors that are identified by management. To mitigate the risk that testing is insufficient, the auditor should include a combination of test types such as inquiries, observation and inspection.
- Issue: The description of the tests of controls is insufficient in detail regarding the nature, timing and extent of testing to permit the user enterprise's management or the auditor to assess the control risk for the financial statement assertions of the user enterprise. In this instance, management and the auditor may be able to arrange a discussion with the service organization and its auditor to obtain additional information regarding the description

of the tests. Such inquiries and the responses should be documented in accordance with standards and an evaluation of the sufficiency of the responses received. If such a discussion cannot be arranged, the specific testing should be treated as providing insufficient evidential matter to support a conclusion.

- Issue: The description of tests that are performed on the relevant aspects of the control environment, information and communication, risk assessment, and monitoring that are related to the services provided is not sufficient to permit the user enterprise's management or the auditor to assess their operating effectiveness in establishing, enhancing or mitigating the effectiveness of the specified controls. Management and the auditor should consider performing limited procedures to test these controls through inquiry and inspection of regulatory filings and other documents.
- Issue: In describing the results of tests of operating effectiveness performed, the description of deviations is not sufficient (e.g., sample size, number of deviations noted, the nature of the deviations, causative factors, corrective actions or other relevant qualitative information) to permit the user enterprise's management or the auditor to assess their impact on the control risk for the financial statement assertions of the user enterprise. In this instance, the user enterprise's management or the auditor may be able to arrange a discussion with the service organization and its auditor to obtain additional information regarding the description of the exception(s).

Such inquiries and the responses should be documented in accordance with standards, and the control should be evaluated based on the response received. If such a discussion cannot be arranged, management and the auditor should consider the control as not operating effectively and should evaluate its impact on the user enterprise's financial statement assertions.

5.8 Qualifications and Deviations

Enterprises often have an obligation to implement specific controls as part of their contract requirements with a vendor and the terms and conditions of the overall outsourcing relationship. A service auditor's report may contain a qualification that requires the enterprise to implement specific controls to achieve the service organization's stated control objectives. The control objectives stated in the description can be achieved only if complementary user entity controls (CUECs) are suitably designed and operating effectively by the user organization in conjunction with the controls at the service organization.

Some examples of CUECs in SOC 1 reports:

- General IT controls, policies and procedures may be required to meet logical access requirements.
- Policies and procedures that ensure transactions are appropriately authorized and transactions are secure, timely and complete may be required.
- Data transmission policies and procedures that require encryption may be expected.

The user organization's external auditors must determine whether they can rely on the SOC 1 report combined with user management's CUECs. The user organization's external auditors must verify whether the enterprise has the necessary CUECs, otherwise the vendor control objectives will not be met.

Following are typical issues:

- Issue: The opinion of the service organization's external auditor reflects internal controls at the service organization that are ineffective. When the service auditor's opinion contains a qualification in the opinion—or an exception is noted in the description of the results of testing—management should identify the qualification or exception as a control deficiency and identify any controls implemented by the user enterprise that compensate for the control deficiency noted. The risk associated with the deficiency should also be mitigated. The deficiency should then be evaluated in accordance with the user enterprise's methodology for evaluating deficiencies.

- Issue: There is insufficient detail on the qualifications contained within the service auditor's opinion to permit the user enterprise's management or the auditor to assess the impact on the control risk for the financial statement assertions of the user enterprise. In this instance, management and the auditor may be able to arrange a discussion with the service organization and its auditor to obtain additional information regarding the description of the qualification. Such inquiries and the responses should be documented in accordance with standards, and the control objective and related controls should be evaluated based on the response received. If such a discussion cannot be arranged, the user enterprise's management and the auditor should consider the control objectives as not having been achieved and should evaluate its impact on the user enterprise's financial statement assertions.

5.9 Service Organization External Auditor

According to AS 2601, the service organization's external auditors are responsible for their report and for exercising due care in the application of procedures that support those representations, including performing the audit with required quality control procedures.[94] A service auditor's engagement should be performed in accordance with the relevant PCAOB auditing standards. The service organization's auditor should be independent of the service organization, but it is not required that the service organization's auditor be independent of each user organization. The following issue regarding the service organization external auditor may arise:

- Issue: The reputation, competence, independence and professional standing of the service organization's external auditor are not sufficient to support the management assessment and the user organization's external auditor's opinion. Where the reputation, competence, independence or professional standing of the service auditor is not sufficient, management and the user organization's external auditor should consider the nature and extent of the procedures that were performed to be insufficient and should perform additional procedures.

AS 2201, paragraph .B23 says that the user organization's external auditor must evaluate the service organization's auditor in the same way the external auditor must evaluate the internal audit function's effectiveness as an entity-level control while planning the audit and its tests and before relying on its work.[95] The external auditor should make inquiries concerning the service auditor's reputation, competence and independence. Appropriate sources of information concerning the professional reputation of the service auditor are discussed in paragraph .10a of AS 1205: *Part of the Audit Performed by Other Independent Auditors*.[96]

This background work may be performed in advance by the internal auditor to reduce the external auditor's effort. The user organization's external auditor, aided by the internal auditor, should consider the guidance in AS 1205, paragraph .12 regarding additional information to be obtained from the service organization auditor, if applicable.[97]

These reports, prepared in accordance with AT-C section 320, *Reporting on an Examination of Controls at a Service Organization Relevant to User Entities' Internal Control Over Financial Reporting*, are specifically intended to meet the needs of the entities that use service organizations (user entities) and the CPAs that audit the user entity's financial statements (user auditors), in evaluating the effect of the controls at the service organization on the user entity's financial statements. Use of these reports is restricted to the management of the service organization, user entities and user auditors. The external auditor does not refer to the service auditor's report when expressing an opinion on the enterprise internal control over financial reporting.

[94] *Op cit* PCAOB, AS 2601: *Consideration of an Entity's Use of a Service Organization*
[95] *Op cit* PCAOB, AS 2201: *An Audit of Internal Control Over Financial Reporting That Is Integrated with An Audit of Financial Statements*
[96] PCAOB, AS 1205: *Part of the Audit Performed by Other Independent Auditors, https://pcaobus.org/oversight/standards/auditing-standards/details/AS1205*
[97] *Ibid.*

5.10 SOC for Cybersecurity

Enterprise management and boards frequently engage information security or cybersecurity consultants to assess cybersecurity risk and recommend improvements. Ideally, this work is performed before a breach or hacking incident occurs. After an incident, the services become crisis-oriented and may be required to put shareholders, customers, employees and other stakeholders at ease and to respond to a remediation requirement resulting from a legal or regulatory settlement. Typically, the services are limited in scope and requested in response to an identified issue. These services can be valuable in any context, but especially if they can offer an independent, enterprisewide perspective on an organization cybersecurity risk management program to the entity stakeholders.

With those challenges in mind, the AICPA determined that stakeholders of an organization—management, directors, investors, analysts, business partners and others—would benefit from an independent assessment of an organization's cybersecurity risk management program, resulting in a report with useful information that can be used to make informed, future-focused decisions.

In April 2017, the AICPA introduced SOC® for Cybersecurity, a cybersecurity risk management examination designed to help all types of organizations meet the growing challenge of communicating to interested parties the design and effectiveness of their cybersecurity risk management programs. Although a SOC 2 report and a SOC for Cybersecurity report can provide users significant perspective and insight into the cybersecurity controls of an organization, there are some meaningful differences between the audience, subject matter and scope of each that serve a variety of critical marketplace needs.[98]

In a SOC for Cybersecurity examination, management of an entity prepares a description of the entity cybersecurity risk management program and makes an assertion about that description and about the effectiveness of controls within the program. In a SOC 2 examination, management of a service organization develops a description of a specific system the service organization uses to process transactions for user entities and makes an assertion about that description and about the effectiveness of controls within that system. The SOC for Cybersecurity examination allows management to select the criteria against which to evaluate the effectiveness of controls to achieve the entity's cybersecurity objectives.

The SOC for Cybersecurity report includes the following:

- A description of the entity cybersecurity risk management program in accordance with the cybersecurity description criteria
- A written assertion by management about whether the description of the entity cybersecurity risk management program was presented in accordance with the cybersecurity description criteria and whether controls within the program were effective in achieving the entity cybersecurity objectives based on the control criteria
- A CPA report that contains an opinion about whether the description of the entity cybersecurity risk management program is presented in accordance with the cybersecurity description criteria and whether controls within the cybersecurity risk management program were effective in achieving the entity cybersecurity objectives based on the control criteria

5.11 Cloud Assurance for CSPs

A technology shift that most practitioners thought would happen over the next five years is happening now because of the COVID-19 pandemic. Enterprises moved quickly to deploy additional digital capabilities to keep businesses open and to connect employees with their work and the enterprise with its customers, employees, vendors and other stakeholders.

[98] AICPA, "SOC 2® examinations and SOC for Cybersecurity examinations: Understanding the key distinctions," 2017, *www.aicpa.org/content/dam/aicpa/interestareas/frc/assuranceadvisoryservices/downloadabledocuments/cybersecurity/soc-2-vs-cyber-whitepaper-web-final.pdf*

As a result, enterprises are now moving to the cloud at a rapid pace via cloud-native solutions, anywhere connectivity and hybrid multicloud architectures. Those solutions must be automated and secure and provide remote capabilities at scale. Data security and privacy challenges in today's cloud-based environments must be addressed.

There are several ways CSPs can provide assurance to their customers.[99] The CSA, in collaboration with the AICPA, developed a third-party assessment program of CSPs called the CSA Security, Trust, Assurance and Risk (STAR) Attestation. STAR incorporates key principles of transparency, rigorous auditing and harmonization of standards.

The SOC 2+ report allows a SOC 2 to report on any additional controls over and above the trust services criteria controls for security, availability, confidentiality, processing integrity and privacy. STAR Attestation leverages this framework to provide CPAs performing independent assessments of CSPs using SOC 2 engagements with the CSA CCM®.

CSA promotes its CCM as the only metaframework of cloud-specific security controls, because it is mapped to leading standards, best practices and regulations. CCM provides organizations with the needed structure, detail and clarity relating to information security tailored to cloud computing. CCM is currently considered a *de facto* standard for cloud security assurance and compliance. STAR Attestation is based on type 1 or type 2 SOC attestations supplemented by the criteria in the CCM.

5.12 How to Evaluate a SOC Report

Following is a checklist for how to evaluate a SOC report.[100]

- Create a current inventory of reports and controls for the service organizations and a checklist for reviewing the reports to ensure all areas are covered. This inventory and checklist will help the enterprise manage risk, respond to external auditors, and make everyone's reviews more efficient and effective.
- Make sure the enterprise has the right report for its needs. Some vendors issue multiple reports for different parts of their businesses and to different types of customers. Only CPA firms can issue SOC reports. Make sure that the firm or individual issuing the report has the correct experience and requisite information technology or information security certifications, such as Certified Information Systems Security Professional (CISSP®), Certified Information Systems Auditor® (CISA®) and Certified in Risk and Information Systems Control® (CRISC®).
- Make sure the time period of the report covers enterprise needs. If there is a gap between the report and the time period required for the review or the external auditor's review, the external auditor may have to conduct additional procedures. Ineffective controls at a key service provider could have serious consequences on the enterprise control environment. Alternatively, the enterprise can obtain a bridge letter.
- Review the management opinion on the operating effectiveness of the controls and the service auditor's opinion. If the two opinions differ, the reason should be investigated. If the auditor provides anything other than an unqualified opinion, there should be a separate paragraph to describe the reasons for the opinion and evaluate the impact of the exceptions. There are four possible ways the auditor can present the opinion:
    - Review the description of the service organization control environment. This description can provide valuable insights for enterprise management, its internal auditors and the external auditor.
    - Note and investigate control exceptions. A high number of exceptions at a mature vendor is a cause for concern. This is especially important for key controls that are relied on to achieve overall control effectiveness.

[99] Chaudhary, A.; "SOC Reports for Cloud Security and Privacy," *ISACA® Journal*, 18 December 2019, *www.isaca.org/resources/isaca-journal/issues/2019/volume-6/soc-reports-for-cloud-security-and-privacy*

[100] Gardner, B.; "How to Properly Review a SOC Report," *ISACA® Now Blog*, 19 June 2019, *www.isaca.org/resources/news-and-trends/isaca-now-blog/2019/how-to-properly-review-an-soc-report*

- Review user control considerations and address discrepancies between the controls the service organization assumes are in place and those that exist and are effective. The section listing controls that should be in place at the user organization are typically called user control considerations, complementary user entity controls or description of client considerations. They may not all be applicable, but this section may provide insight and may point out gaps in the enterprise control structure.
- Determine if the enterprise relies on a subservice and if a report is needed from the subservice provider, or if the enterprise needs to perform any other investigations. Service providers may be outsourcing part of the service they provide to the enterprise, such as hosting or the help desk. The report should list any activities that are outsourced.

Page intentionally left blank

Chapter 6

IT Sarbanes-Oxley Compliance Road Map

6.1 Introduction

This chapter provides a compliance road map that meets the objectives and responsibilities of IT in support of ICFR. Understanding how SOX compliance applies to an enterprise—based on its business characteristics—aids in the development of the enterprise's internal control program. Many functional units within IT come into play in ensuring appropriate compliance with SOX. Larger enterprises face challenges in the application of SOX that are distinct from those of smaller enterprises. Also, the extent to which a strong internal control framework is already in place has significant bearing on financial reporting activities.

The road map, illustrated in **figure 6.1**, provides direction for business, finance and IT professionals to meet the challenges of SOX compliance. Six stages in the road map can take the enterprise to a level of sustainable compliance. Enterprises normally undertake the first two stages in the road map—planning and scoping of IT controls and the assessment of IT risk—in tandem. The enterprise then documents these controls and evaluates the design and effectiveness of controls.

Figure 6.1—IT SOX Compliance Road Map

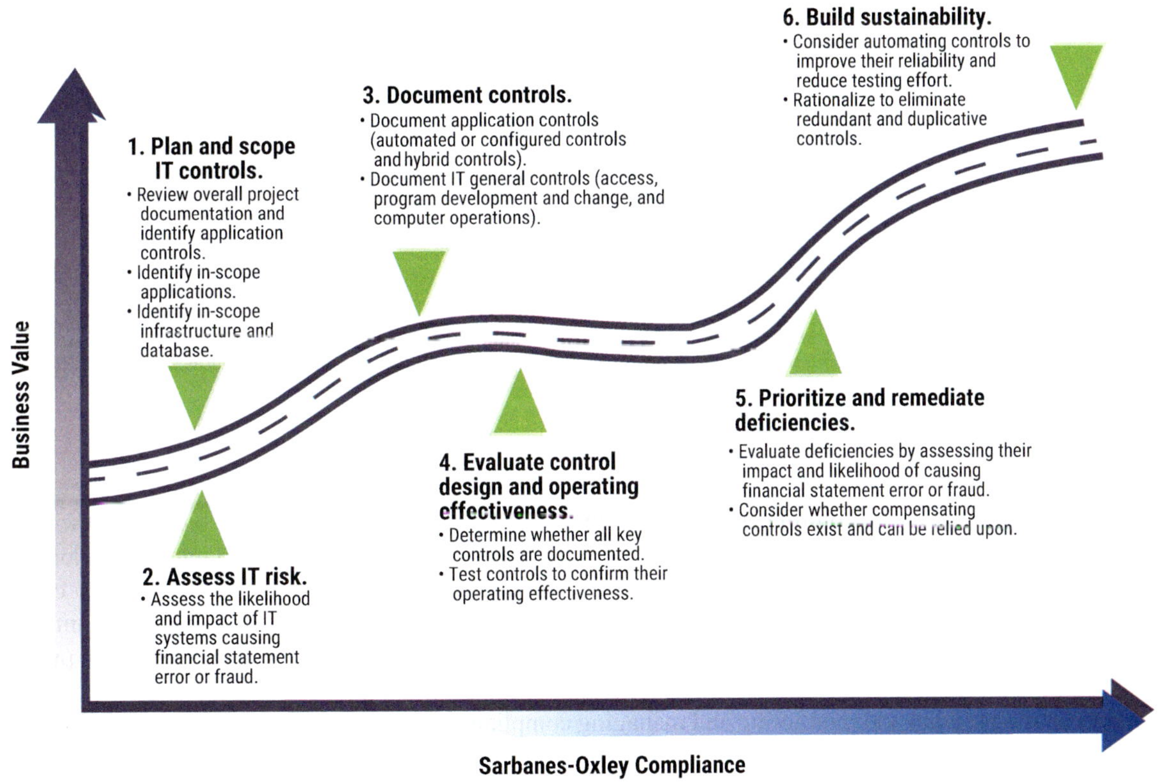

Source: Adapted from ISACA, *IT Control Objectives for Sarbanes-Oxley: Using COBIT® 5 in the Design and Implementation of Internal Controls Over Financial Reporting*, 3rd Edition, USA, 2014, *https://store.isaca.org/s/store#/store/browse/detail/a2S4w000004Ko9JEAS*

6.2 Step 1. Plan and Scope Application and IT Controls

Like all IT control compliance programs, careful attention should be given to properly scoping and planning the SOX compliance program. Scoping is the process of understanding those IT applications and subsystems that are included in the review and those that are excluded from the review. IT should work with and use the findings of the finance and business teams to make these judgments. The inclusion and exclusion of applications and subsystems flow from the overall financial risk assessment process of the enterprise. Finance and business compliance teams lead this process. Only those applications and related subsystems that support business and relevant controls over financial reporting should be in scope. A further discussion and example are provided in Sections 6.2.1 through 6.2.8. **Figure 6.2** provides a top-down scoping process for an IT control program.

Figure 6.2—Scoping the IT Control Project—Top Down

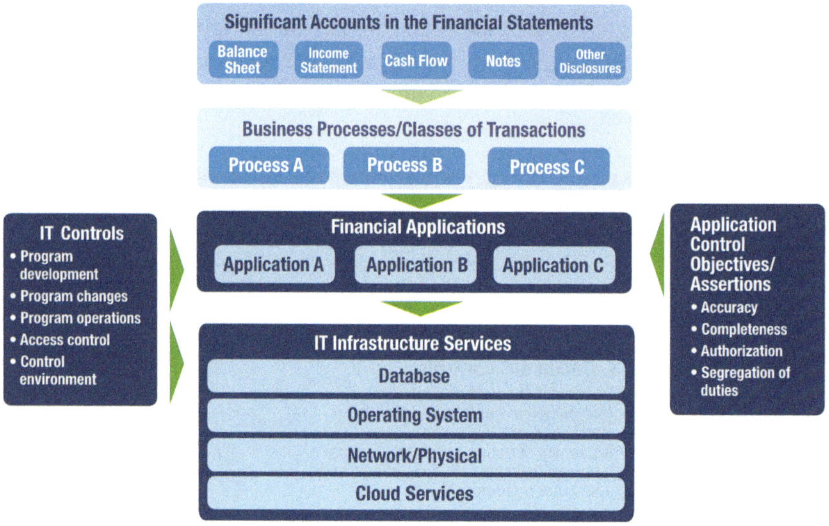

Source: Adapted from ISACA, *IT Control Objectives for Sarbanes-Oxley: Using COBIT® 5 in the Design and Implementation of Internal Controls Over Financial Reporting, 3rd Edition*, USA, 2014, *https://store.isaca.org/s/store#/store/browse/detail/a2S4w000004Ko9JEAS*

6.2.1 Assign Accountability and Responsibility

An important first step in the IT control compliance program, for enterprises that become subject to SOX compliance, is to form an IT control subcommittee. The subcommittee should be integrated into, and report to, the overall Sarbanes-Oxley steering committee. The IT subcommittee should oversee the IT Sarbanes-Oxley compliance program and facilitate communication and integration with the finance and business control teams, and internal and external auditors. The subcommittee should appoint an IT compliance manager to be responsible for the program and ongoing compliance activities. The IT compliance manager should be given appropriate authority and accountability for completing the program and monitoring and managing compliance on an ongoing basis.

6.2.2 Inventory Relevant Applications and Related Subsystems

An inventory of in-scope applications and technology infrastructure should be developed and maintained. An example is shown in Appendix D. The IT compliance manager works with the finance and business controls team to make decisions on which applications and subsystems are in scope. Typically, applications that support online authorizations, complex calculations, or valuations, or are responsible for maintaining the integrity of significant account balances, such as inventory, fixed assets or loan balances, should be identified in this phase. An inventory of in-scope applications and subsystems is not a static record. It must be updated when required. This is a continuous activity; any new application or subsystem entering enterprise architecture needs to undergo the review to decide whether it is required to be in scope. There needs to be intensive review of the application or subsystem to determine all applicable controls. The IT compliance manager also needs to review and update inventory in case there is any application or subsystem that is no longer supporting the business. Chapter 4 provides more guidance on application controls and application control objectives. This is supported by Appendix C, Example Application Controls.

By having such an inventory of applications, the IT control program team should be able to identify all applications that need to be considered and identify all subsystems that support the applications, including databases, servers, operating systems and networks.

6.2.3 Determine the IT General Controls That Are in Scope

Not all the ITGCs that are outlined in Appendix A will be in scope or have the same priority. It is important to include ITGCs with applications in the risk assessment phase (step 2 of the road map). It is also important for this step 1 to accomplish:

- Understanding the enterprise's internal control program and its financial reporting processes
- Identifying the IT systems involved in the initiation, authorization, processing, summarization and reporting of financial data
- Identifying the key controls that address specific financial risk. Appendix A gives a recommendation of key control areas (KCAs) and provides suggestions that are identified with a star (✯).

The design and implementation of ITGCs should be done to address the identified risk of the organization financial reporting. The appropriate approach[101] for identifying the exact scope and extent of testing for SOX ITGCs is to perform a detailed risk assessment that is focused on the risk that is associated with each general control process area, such as change management, logical access, computer operations, job scheduling, and third parties/service organizations that manage applications or data centers.

6.2.4 Consider Multilocation Issues

Among the many factors in scoping the IT control program are enterprises with multiple subsidiary companies, decentralized operations and cloud-based/on-premises operations. This is particularly challenging for those enterprises that have dispersed locations (domestic/international). The SOX audit program needs to include in the audit plan resourcing and costs for undertaking an audit of internal controls at these locations.

6.2.5 Identify Dependencies on Third-Party Service Organizations

Some enterprises use external service organizations to perform outsourced services. These services are still part of overall enterprise operations and responsibility and, consequently, need to be considered in the overall IT internal control program. According to AS 2201:

> *If the service organization's services are part of a company's information system, as described therein, then they are part of the information and communication component of the company's internal control over financial reporting. When the service organization's services are part of the company's internal control over financial reporting, the auditor should include the activities of the service organization when determining the evidence required to support his or her opinion.*[102]

[101] Mehta, A.; "An Approach Toward Sarbanes-Oxley ITGC Risk Assessment," *ISACA® Journal* Archives, 1 September 2010, *www.isaca.org/resources/isaca-journal/past-issues/2010/an-approach-toward-sarbanes-oxley-itgc-risk-assessment*

[102] *Op cit* PCAOB, AS 2201: *An Audit of Internal Control Over Financial Reporting That Is Integrated with An Audit of Financial Statements*

See Chapter 5, Using Service Organization Reports for ICFR.

6.2.6 Consider IT-Based Antifraud Controls

IT-based antifraud controls under SOX are critical to protect from eventual internal and external crime. Fraud is the principal reason for the introduction of SOX legislation. Sufficient and appropriate attention to this issue is needed.

IT plays a significant role in the prevention and detection of fraud because many antifraud controls rely on automated controls. The following examples of IT-based antifraud controls are relevant for inclusion in an enterprise's SOX compliance program:

- **Application-enforced segregation of duties**—Most application systems have the ability to define the privileges that are assigned to users within the application. As a result, the system enforces appropriate approvals for transaction processing and prevents users from initiating and authorizing their own transactions.
- **Access controls**—Most systems have privileged users who can access sensitive information, such as payroll data. These privileged users are able to add fictitious employees and thereby commit fraud. Limiting such access to a few people and making sure that the financial reporting team does not have this access is important to establishing ICFR.

Segregation of duties (SoD) is a key internal control and regulates which users have access to what areas of applications and IT infrastructure. The purpose of segregating responsibilities is to prevent occupational fraud in the form of asset misappropriation and intentional financial misstatement. The core concept that underlies SoD is that no employee or group of employees should be in a position to perpetrate and conceal errors or fraud in the normal course of their duties. In general, duties to be segregated are:

- Custody of assets
- Authorization or approval of related transactions affecting those assets
- Recording or reporting of related transactions
- Verification

Example: Order to Pay

Below is an example of SoD using the order-to-pay process. This process is about the management of suppliers and third parties, setting up a master file of suppliers, processing purchase orders, processing purchase invoices and paying purchase invoices. The key SoD principle is that no one role should have access to all processes. Most especially, the person who processes the invoice should not approve payment of the invoice. Duties should typically be segregated into:

- Initiation and authorization of purchase orders
- Processing of purchase invoices (in many applications this is now automated—preventive controls)
- Payment of invoices
- Managing supplier master files

None of these roles should have access to the same application functionality. For example, the person managing the master file data (creating, amending, etc.) should not be allowed to process an invoice or pay an invoice.

6.2.7 Develop a Preliminary Program Plan and Obtain Approval

Using the inventory of in-scope applications and subsystems, a preliminary program plan of activities should be developed using the six phases described in **figure 6.1**. The program plan will be modified and refined later, but it is important to get an overall view of the program's size and approach.

After the plan is developed, it is important to discuss with the finance and business controls compliance team the in-scope applications and appropriateness of the program's scope. Once this process is complete, it is time to obtain approval to proceed with the program. Obtaining formal approval is very important, given the significance of the program and the impact it will have on various members of the enterprise. Formal approval solidifies the sponsors of the program and allows one to obtain buy-in from all relevant stakeholders and staff members who need to participate.

6.3 Step 2. Assess IT Risk

In this phase, enterprises need to assess risk within the IT processes and subsystems that support the applications in scope. One of the most significant lessons learned through the initial years of SOX compliance programs is that the program must be risk-based.

6.3.1 Assess the Risk of Applications and Related Subsystems

Assessment of the risk of applications and their related subsystems, such as databases, operating systems, networks and physical environments, is necessary to determine the nature and extent of controls that are needed to manage such risk. It is also necessary to understand the risk of application and related subsystems to properly plan and perform testing of operating effectiveness of such controls. Although performing a risk assessment requires consideration of several risk factors, the final assessment of relative risk requires judgment. The purpose of considering common risk factors is to provide enterprises with relevant information for the development of a relative risk assessment. The risk assessment considers the probability and impact of the risk event. Without controls, the likelihood of this happening is not entirely remote, and the impact of entering false transactions is significant. As a result, this risk is significant, and controls are required to reduce the risk.

AS 2201, paragraph .B31 specifically addresses the concept of benchmarking for lower-risk applications with automated controls. The standard states:

> *To determine whether to use a benchmarking strategy, the auditor should assess the following risk factors. As these factors indicate lower risk, the control being evaluated might be well-suited for benchmarking. As these factors indicate increased risk, the control being evaluated is less suited for benchmarking. These factors are:*
>
> - *The extent to which the application control can be matched to a defined program within an application.*
> - *The availability and reliability of a report of the compilation dates of the programs placed in production. (This information may be used as evidence that controls within the program have not changed.)*[103]

AS 2201 further states the following in paragraph .B32:

> *Benchmarking automated application controls can be especially effective for companies using purchased software when the possibility of program changes is remote – e.g., when the vendor does not allow access or modification to the source code.*[104]

The following risk factors are often relevant in the conduct of the risk assessment. Enterprises should determine whether other risk factors are relevant, based on their unique circumstances:

- Nature of technology (complex or simple)

[103] *Ibid.*
[104] *Ibid.*

- Nature of people (experienced or inexperienced)
- Nature of processes (centralized or decentralized)
- Past experience
- Significance to the financial statements

AS 2201 requires the user organization's external auditor to test those entity-level controls that are important to the auditor's conclusion about whether the company has effective ICFR. Entity-level controls include centralized processing and controls included in shared service environments. Third-party service organizations must have effective and transparent information technology controls over internal and outsourced functions. These vendors must be able to prove to their customers—the organizations that outsource key activities or functions to the service organizations—that controls are in place, operating effectively and can be relied on. However, company management remains accountable for controls over these activities despite delegating these tasks or functions to a service organization. Enterprise management is ultimately accountable to the board of directors, customers, shareholders, regulators and others for the accurate, timely and authorized processing of enterprise data.

The enterprise's approach to SOX risk assessment should identify the key risk parameters that will help to quantify the risk for ITGCs. An application might be considered high risk when viewed from a change management perspective because it might undergo hundreds of changes every month; but it might be low risk when viewed from a logical access perspective because it has only four to five administrators and no end users accessing the application.

Although this publication does not focus on how risk assessments should be undertaken, *COBIT Focus Area: Information and Technology Risk Using COBIT 2019* is highly recommended for the information about generic risk scenarios in its Appendix A, I&T Risk Scenarios[105] and the examples that are outlined in figure A.1 of that publication. These relate easily to the SOX control objectives that are outlined in this publication.

This is not a replacement for a full risk assessment but complements and assists the auditors in linking specific risk scenarios to the control objectives outlined in Appendix A. **Figure 6.3** shows risk scenarios from *COBIT Focus Area: Information and Technology Risk Using COBIT 2019*. These are linked to the specific COBIT process control objectives and activities in Appendix A.

[105] *Op cit* ISACA, *COBIT Focus Area: Information and Technology Risk*

Figure 6.3—Example Risk Scenarios

I&T Risk Scenario Category[106]		Example Scenarios—Primary Impacts			COBIT 2019 and General IT Control Objectives	
		Example Generic I&T Risk Scenarios		Example Specific I&T Risk Scenarios	COBIT 2019 Reference	Control Reference and Control Objective
10	Internal and external security threats (hacker, malware, etc.)	A	Unauthorized (internal) users successfully break into systems.	An internal user breaks into a key business application and deletes customer account information.	DSS05.04 DSS06.03	**Appendix A, figure A.12** Procedures exist and are followed to authenticate all users of the system (both internal and external) to support the existence of transactions.
		B	Service interruption occurs due to a denial of service (DoS) attack.	A distributed denial of service (DDoS) attack results in performance degradation of a key business website.	DSS05.01 DSS05.02 DSS05.03	**Appendix A, figure A.12** Appropriate controls, including firewalls, intrusion detection and vulnerability assessments, exist and are used to prevent unauthorized access via public networks.

Given the PCAOB move to a risk-based approach in AS 2201, discussed in Chapter 2, most enterprises have moved to combine their previous COBIT 2019 control templates with the risk ranking results of their risk assessments. Use of an ITGC SOX control matrix (CM) facilitates this process. Appendix E shows an example CM using the same security control objective information that is shown in the risk scenario example in **figure 6.3**.

The main purpose of the CM is to present a complete in-scope picture of all ITGCs for a particular enterprise. It is a master control document for the client or sponsor. It is not a risk register or a risk assessment; it links or cross-references the risk findings resulting from ranking and prioritization.

The second purpose is to summarize test findings that are cross-referenced to the audit documentation.

Note

The example shown in **figure 6.3** is incomplete; to provide a full example is not possible here because these templates can potentially include many columns and many pages of information.[107]

6.3.2 Determine the Applications That Are in Scope

This step cannot be started until the risk assessment in step 2 has been undertaken. This scoping process is an important consideration, particularly for enterprises that run many applications, and especially for those with custom systems. A key part of the risk assessment should consider the following factors:

- Volume of transactions processed
- Value amount of the transactions
- Complexity of any calculations
- Sensitivity of data and transactions
- Quantitative materiality

[106] Adapted from *COBIT Focus Area: Information and Technology Risk*, figure A.1, mapped to general IT control objectives for Sarbanes-Oxley
[107] *Op cit* ISACA, *COBIT® Focus Area: Information and Technology Risk*

Figure 6.4 provides an example of in-scope applications and their risk ranking.

Figure 6.4—Example of In-scope Applications

A medium-size manufacturing enterprise uses SAP as its main ERP system but has three major custom systems: inventory/work in progress (WIP) tracking, transport dispatch and machinery maintenance. All are interfaced to the SAP® system. All SoD work product application controls are automated, including interface controls to SAP.

Applications	Impact on Financial Reporting	Risk	Audit Priority and Comments
SAP	• General ledger financial reporting • Order to pay • Order to cash • Payroll	High	Top priority
Inventory/WIP	The SAP stock module is not used. All quantity and stock valuations are done in this application.	High	Top priority, because it affects the valuation of stock and WIP in the general ledger
Transport dispatch	Logistical tracking of trucks dispatched and driver hours are interfaced to SAP payroll and SAP projects.	Medium	Second-tier priority, because it affects payroll costs, which, in this case, are charged to transportation costs. The subsystem does no cost calculation.
Machinery maintenance	Machinery tracking and maintenance schedule application tracks only machine hours for scheduled maintenance. Only engineer schedules interface to the SAP project module.	Low	Third-tier priority, because there is no valuation; maintenance hours are part of SAP payroll and project feed.

This step in the program also helps the IT organization to gain an understanding of how the financial reporting process works and identify where technology is critical in the support of the business processes.

The inventory of applications and related subsystems is a primary input to risk assessment and preliminary planning. The inventory is a key input to the risk assessment stage to determine the nature and extent of controls and testing required.

6.3.3 Refine Scope and Update the Program Plan

After completion of the risk assessment, the IT controls team should be able to refine the program scope and update the applications and related subsystems that are in scope and out of scope. Documentation of the risk assessment process and related conclusions is important, particularly where systems are out of scope. Similarly, the program plan should be updated where changes to scope and the extent of effort is modified to reflect a risk-based approach.

6.4 Step 3. Document Controls

This section focuses on the technique of how to document the controls that are identified as in-scope in the previous steps. The purpose of this section is to give guidance on tools that help enterprises, especially those enterprises that are complying with SOX for the first time.

6.4.1 Document Application Controls

Chapter 4 and Appendix C provide details to assist enterprises in the documentation of application controls. It is not a complete list of examples.

6.4.2 Document Entity and IT General Controls

Chapter 2 provides details on COBIT 2019 mapped to the PCAOB AS 2201 requirements. This mapping was developed into a detailed listing for SOX compliance, which is provided in Appendix A, Entity-level/Activity-level and IT General Controls for Sarbanes-Oxley. Within these lists, certain controls are key controls, which are indicated by a star (✯) in Appendix A. This marking shows that these are the most commonly used controls in designing a reliable and robust IT general control environment.

6.4.3 Use a Control Documentation Template

Under the SOX Act, enterprises are required to document controls over financial reporting and perform an assessment of their design and operating effectiveness. Documentation may take various forms. These include entity policy manuals, IT policies and procedures, narratives, flowcharts, decision tables, procedural write-ups, and completed questionnaires. The breadth and depth of documentation may vary, depending on the size and complexity of the enterprise. A template with an example for the documentation of the design of IT controls is in Appendix F.

For most enterprises, documentation of the ITGCs should include:

- **Controls narrative**—Documentation of the design of the controls, which includes:
    - IT general controls (categorized by COSO as activity controls)
    - Description of the processes and related subprocesses. This may be in narrative form but may be more effective to illustrate as a flowchart.
    - Description of the risk ranking and whether it is a key control area (taken from the risk control matrix [RCM])
    - Statement of the control objective that is designed to reduce the risk of the process or subprocess to an acceptable level (shown in Appendix A)
    - The type of controls (preventive or detective) and frequency
    - Conclusions reached about the effectiveness of the design of the controls
    - An SoD chart by process/control area
- **Test documentation**: (Note that an example template is not provided.)
    - Description of the approach followed to test the existence and operational effectiveness of the control activities
    - The control activities to test (shown in Appendix A)
    - Conclusions reached about the operating effectiveness of the tested control activities

  Test documentation is important, because the narrative documentation may show that the control is well designed and in place. The testing may show that it has not been applied or is poorly applied, which will create a deficiency, significant deficiency or material weakness.
- **Entity level**—Assessment of entity-level controls, including evidence to support the responses and opinions of management. An example questionnaire is provided in Appendix A.

6.5 Evaluate Control Design and Operating Effectiveness

When controls are being designed, management needs to evaluate the appropriateness of the controls: Are they preventive, detective, automated or manual? For example, a properly designed control could prevent the risk that arises from change management that could result in unauthorized programs being migrated into the production environment. In this example, a detective control that identifies unauthorized programs in production after the fact may not be appropriate, given the risk involved.

Analysis of control design in the overall IT control environment is crucial. AS 2201 points out the importance of IT controls and reinforces the notion that such controls are necessary to support the overall internal control environment. In particular, AS 2201 states that the effectiveness of an enterprise's overall system of internal control is dependent on the effectiveness of other controls. These controls include the control environment and ITGCs. Accordingly, the evaluation of control design is an essential step in evaluating the IT control environment.

The COBIT process assessment model employs the ISO/IEC 33000 Process Capability Model.[108] (See **figure 6.5**.) There is no specific stage required for SOX compliance other than a requirement for documentation and testing of controls. Enterprises should carefully consider at which stage (process capability) they are currently and whether this presents a risk to SOX compliance.

In COBIT 2019, the explicit process outcomes or process goals are replaced by the process practices themselves. This results in the following situation for an ISO/IEC33000 evaluation:

- Process outcomes are now linked to the process practices on a one-to-one basis (i.e., the process outcomes are the successful completion of the process practices). Note: The process practices are formulated as practices, and the outcomes can be derived from there. Example: APO01.01 *Design the management system for enterprise I&T* has as process outcome APO01.01: *A management system for enterprise I&T is designed.*
- Base practices are equal to the COBIT 2019 process practices for each governance and management objective.
- Work products are equal to the Information Flows and Items under Component C in each governance/management objective.

Thus, the mapping of outcomes to base practices and work products is all done by definition in COBIT 2019:

> *If enterprises desire to continue using the COBIT 5 process capability model based on International Organization for Standardization (ISO)/International Electrotechnical Commission (IEC) 15504 (now ISO/IEC 33000, in which capability levels have very different meanings), they have all required information to do so in* COBIT® 2019 Framework: Governance and Management Objectives. *No separate process assessment model (PAM) publications are necessary, nor will they be provided with COBIT® 2019.*[109]

[108] ISACA, *COBIT® Process Assessment Model (PAM): Using COBIT® 5*, USA, 2013, *https://store.isaca.org/s/store#/store/browse/detail/a2S4w000004Ko9NEAS*

[109] ISACA, *COBIT® 2019 Framework: Introduction and Methodology*, USA, 2018, *https://store.isaca.org/s/store#/store/browse/detail/a2S4w000004Ko9cEAC*

Figure 6.5—Capability Levels for Processes

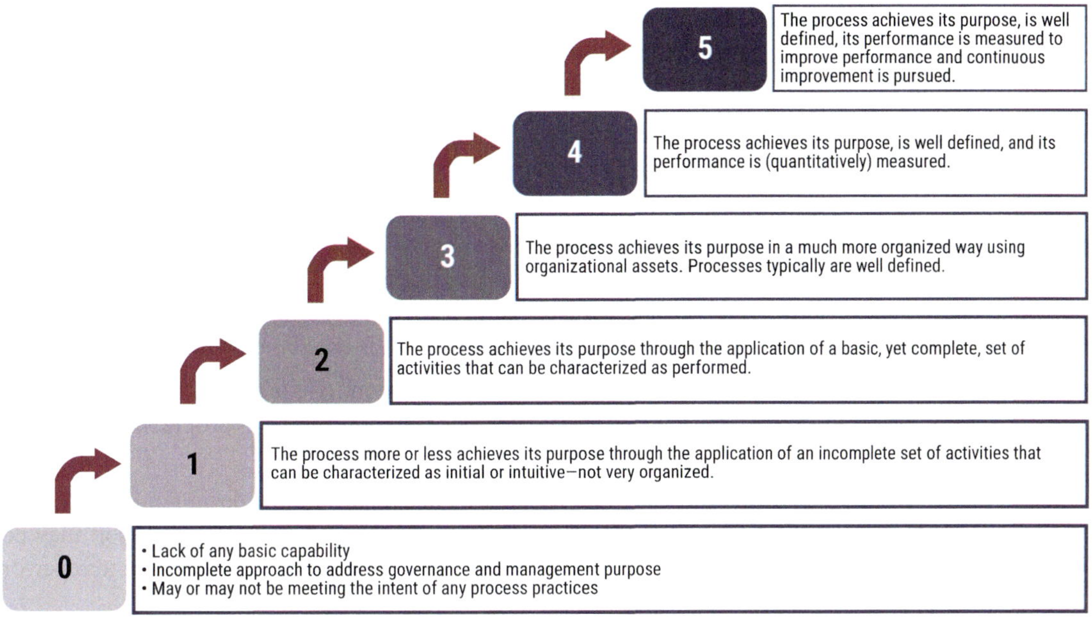

Source: ISACA, *COBIT® 2019 Framework: Introduction and Methodology*, USA, 2018, *https://store.isaca.org/s/store#/store/browse/detail/a2S4w000004Ko9cEAC*

6.5.1 Evaluate Operational Effectiveness

When control design has been assessed, as appropriate, its effectiveness should also be tested. During this stage, initial and ongoing tests—conducted by individuals who are responsible for the controls and the internal control program management team—should be performed to test the design and operating effectiveness of the control activities.

Management needs to document its tests of operating effectiveness and conclusions on whether the relevant controls evaluated by management are operating as designed. Similar to the management documentation of its evaluation of control design, management needs to document its evaluation of operational effectiveness in sufficient detail for external auditors to reperform the operational effectiveness tests that were performed by management.

In addition to the information that is documented in the control design evaluation, the documentation of operational effectiveness may include the following information:

- Nature, timing and extent of test steps performed
- Results from testing
- Individual who performed the test and the date performed
- Sample size and test population, where applicable
- Reference and location of supporting documentation
- Conclusion on operational effectiveness
- Exceptions identified and related remediation plans and/or compensating controls

6.5.2 Consider the Nature of Evidence Required

AS 2201 describes different forms of evidence that can be obtained when testing the design and operating effectiveness of controls. In principle, enterprises are expected to obtain a mix of inquiries of appropriate personnel, inspection of relevant documentation, observation of operations and reperformance of the application of the control. Forms of evidence include:

- **Inquiry**—A procedure that consists of seeking information from knowledgeable persons throughout the enterprise. For most enterprises, inquiry is used extensively and is often complemented by performing other procedures.
- **Inspection of documentation**—Because inquiry alone does not provide sufficient evidence to support the design or operating effectiveness of a control, additional tests are necessary. To obtain sufficient evidence about the operating effectiveness of the control, enterprises should corroborate inquiries by performing other procedures, such as inspection of reports or other documentation that is used in performance of the control.
- **Observation**—In circumstances in which documentary evidence of controls or the performance of controls does not exist and is not expected to exist, enterprises should corroborate inquiries of appropriate personnel with observation of enterprise activities.
- **Re-performance**—In circumstances where the quality of evidence regarding the design or effective operation of controls might not be sufficiently persuasive—for example, the signature on an exception report may not be sufficient to demonstrate that all exceptions have been investigated—enterprises may choose to reperform the control, independently run the exception report and investigate exceptions.

6.5.3 Consider the Timing of Control Testing

Enterprises should perform tests of controls over a period of time that is adequate to determine whether, as of the date specified in the management report, the controls necessary for achieving the objectives of the control criteria are operating effectively. The period of time over which enterprises perform tests of controls varies with the nature of the controls being tested and with the frequency with which specific controls operate and specific policies are applied. Some controls operate continuously (e.g., approval of user access requests), while others operate only at certain times (e.g., periodic review of user access lists).

6.5.4 Roll-forward Testing

For many enterprises, the testing of IT controls is performed at an interim date (prior to year-end). When testing controls at an interim date, the IT controls team should determine the additional evidence to obtain concerning the operation of the control for the remaining period. In making that determination, the team should consider:

- Specific controls tested prior to the "as of" date and the results of those tests
- Degree to which evidence about the operating effectiveness of those controls was obtained
- Length of the remaining period
- Possibility that there have been any significant changes in ICFR after the interim date

6.6 Step 5. Prioritize and Remediate Deficiencies

Enterprises need to address two types of deficiencies:

- **Design deficiencies**—Issues that are related to missing controls, inadequate controls, lack of supporting documentation or other flaws in control design that do not sufficiently mitigate the related risk
- **Operating effectiveness deficiencies**—Issues relating to the consistency with which controls are operating, such as not performing a control as designed consistently throughout the year

6.6.1 Consider Guidance From the PCAOB

The nature of IT systems, processes and controls can affect how ITGC deficiencies will be evaluated by the external auditor and, therefore, what it will take for internal auditors to support management in remediating them.

The AS 2201 guidance that is introduced in Chapter 2 includes PCAOB guidance incorporated in Staff Practice Alerts that were published after the introduction of the predecessor standard, AS 5. The severity of a deficiency does not depend on whether a misstatement has occurred but rather on whether there is a reasonable possibility that the enterprise's controls will fail to prevent or detect a misstatement. Thus, the deficiency priority, in terms of remediation, depends on the magnitude of possibility of failure to detect a misstatement and the magnitude of the impact of the potential misstatement if it occurs.

PCAOB Staff Practice Alert No. 11, from 2013, explains how external auditors view the severity of ITGC deficiencies.[110] A deficient IT control might not be inhibiting the prevention or detection of misstatements by itself, but it might impair the effectiveness of important IT-dependent controls. Deficient IT controls might also impair the effectiveness of multiple controls across multiple accounts. In that case, internal auditors may need to assess the severity of those impaired controls in combination across all affected accounts and with other control deficiencies affecting those accounts, before developing a plan for remediation.

6.6.2 Consider the Aggregate Effect of Deficiencies

A cluster of IT control deficiencies may affect the same financial statement account balance or disclosure and, therefore, may be designated as a material weakness. In some cases, individual control deficiencies may be considered insignificant when viewed in isolation, but when combined with other similar deficiencies, may be more significant. For example, an enterprise that does not perform a periodic review of user access lists to its financial application is normally considered to have a control design deficiency. On its own, the deficiency may not be significant, especially if compensating controls exist. However, if this enterprise also failed to properly authorize user access requests for the same application, the aggregate effect of the two deficiencies may result in a significant deficiency or material weakness. The combined effect of control deficiencies related to user access requests and user access reviews can place into question the validity of user access within the financial application and, therefore, place into question the validity of transactions within the system as well. Each deficiency is prioritized higher for remediation, even though each deficiency individually may appear to be less severe.

Figure 6.6 outlines a sample deficiency evaluation decision tree, which can be used to assist in the evaluation of control design or operating effectiveness issues. Enterprises should consult with financial compliance teams and, ultimately, with their senior executive officers before concluding whether a control deficiency is a significant deficiency or a material weakness.

[110] PCAOB, "Staff Audit Practice Alert No. 11: Considerations for Audits of Internal Control Over Financial Reporting," 24 October 2013, *https://pcaob-assets.azureedge.net/pcaob-dev/docs/default-source/standards/qanda/10-24-2013_sapa_11.pdf?sfvrsn=a59f5001_0*

Figure 6.6—Sample Deficiency Evaluation Decision Tree

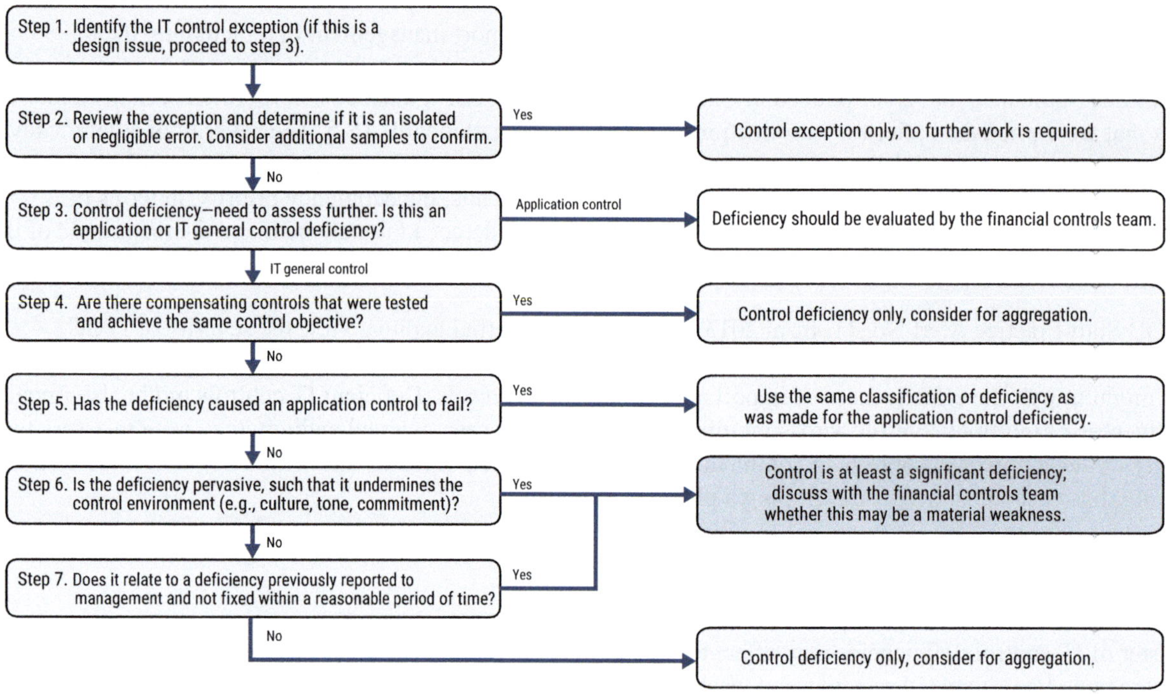

Source: Adapted from ISACA, *IT Control Objectives for Sarbanes-Oxley: Using COBIT® 5 in the Design and Implementation of Internal Controls Over Financial Reporting, 3rd Edition*, USA, 2014, *https://store.isaca.org/s/store#/store/browse/detail/a2S4w000004Ko9JEAS*

6.6.3 Remediate Control Deficiencies

The remediation phase of most programs is where significant effort and money are expended. It is recommended that a remediation log be used to show the risk ranking and help to prioritize the remediation activities. Appendix G provides an example of a remediation log.

The log also shows who is responsible and accountable for remediating control deficiencies. The COBIT 2019 RACI charts for each of the 40 COBIT 2019 governance and management objectives are very useful in assigning responsibility and accountability. In some cases, there may be short-term options for remediation that may not be expensive to implement and can be implemented quickly but may cost more to operate. For example, the manual process for adding, changing and deleting users in systems is time-consuming and slow. However, a long-term solution may include process automation that restricts user access provisioning without appropriate authorization. This approach is more costly in the near term but tends to be more reliable and cost-effective in the long term.

6.7 Step 6. Build Sustainability

At this point, IT management should be able to assess the IT internal control program effectiveness for Sarbanes-Oxley compliance. Effective internal controls, control assessment and management competencies should become part of the IT department organization and culture and sustain themselves over the long term.

Control does not constitute an event. Rather, it is a process that requires continuous support and evaluation to stay current. The ultimate objective is to convert the IT control program into a process. The following activities should be considered to achieve sustained compliance:

- Perform a postimplementation review of the Sarbanes-Oxley compliance program, identifying what went right and areas for improvement.
- Review recent SEC and PCAOB guidance and speeches to determine whether changes in interpretation could impact the future approach.
- Review other independent material for suggestions and opportunities to improve the approach.
- Meet with peers in other enterprises to discuss potential improvements to the process.
- Assess longer-term solutions to address Sarbanes-Oxley issues, such as automation of processes and implementation of program change control software.
- Develop a preliminary plan and timetable for the following year, making it an ingrained process.
- Build the Sarbanes-Oxley process into wider IT governance initiatives.

6.7.1 Rationalize Controls

Control rationalization is another initiative that should take place in the sustainment phase. Some controls will become less useful as technology, business conditions and risk assessments change over time. Enterprises should periodically review their controls to identify which controls can be eliminated from their RCM. While doing so, consideration should be given to the impact of removing a control and any documentation prepared—explaining the rationale about why the control was removed.

Control rationalization does not always mean elimination of controls due to changes in the business environment or new technology. It may also mean introducing new controls that are required due to acquisitions, changes in the risk environment or changes in risk tolerance.

6.7.2 Automate Controls

In most enterprises, a significant number of manual controls can be automated. The application control examples that are provided in Appendix C and Chapter 4 of this publication are a starting point for identifying where to transform manual controls into automated controls. In many cases, more detailed information is needed, depending on the applications available to an enterprise and the nature of controls that are desired. Some enterprises have more detailed control benchmarks that provide such details for a given application, such as SAP and Oracle® NetSuite®.

6.7.3 Consider Ongoing Self-Assessment of IT General Controls

Lessons learned show the importance of enterprises including a self-assessment process in their ongoing monitoring of the effectiveness of their ITGCs. Self-assessment adds value to areas where automation of controls is not possible. Ongoing self-assessment helps in timely detection and remediation of events of ITGC failures. The self-assessment process is usually built into web-based tools and online systems. This is particularly important for lower risk control areas.

Page intentionally left blank

Chapter 7
New Technology Affecting ICFR

7.1 Introduction

Technological innovations, such as big data, cloud computing, virtual supply chains and artificial intelligence, and a universal dependence on Internet connectivity are having a profound effect on financial reporting and disclosure at enterprises. The speed and direction of change, especially after the COVID-19 pandemic period, is having a significant impact on enterprises and their assurance activities. This trend changes the way that auditors—internal and external—support management in ensuring the timeliness, accuracy and integrity of financial statements. Emerging technologies are making digital transformation in leading-edge enterprises possible. These transformational technologies seek to meet the chronic goal of minimizing or eliminating manual tasks and streamlining financial reporting to achieve real-time information access, internally and externally.

7.2 External Auditor Use of Technology Tools

The PCAOB five-year strategic plan for 2020-2024 includes an update on the regulator's Data and Technology Research Project[111] established in December 2016. The PCAOB added the project to its research agenda to understand current and emerging practices in the use of data and technology in audits and to explore whether there is a need for guidance, changes to PCAOB auditing standards or other actions as a result of auditors' use of data and technology.

Audit firms are following the lead of their clients in utilizing the latest technology offerings in their audit process. Some audit firms have established shared service centers or other specialist groups that develop and support the use of technology-based tools on individual audits. These centralized resources may, for example, extract, aggregate, analyze, format and disseminate information to engagement teams in support of their audit procedures.

Some audit firms are using technology-based tools, such as robotic process automation (RPA), to automate certain aspects of repetitive or less complex audit procedures. For example, RPA may be used to reconcile account balances to the general ledger, vouch sales transactions to subsequent cash receipts or prepare confirmations to be sent to third parties. Other firms are also using optical character recognition software to review enterprise documents for keywords selected by the auditor. Examples include lease agreements for payment terms, contracts for unusual terms and conditions, and notes to the financial statements for changes from prior periods.

The PCAOB research project focuses on furthering its understanding about how auditors use technology-based tools to respond to the identified risk of material misstatement. The work reported on in a 2021 update included analyzing the requirements of certain PCAOB standards including AS 2301: *The Auditor's Responses to the Risks of Material Misstatement*; AS 2310: *The Confirmation Process*; and AS 2510: *Auditing Inventories* in the context of the evolving use of technology-based tools. The PCAOB added a project related to audit evidence to its research agenda in late 2020 related to AS 1105: *Audit Evidence*.[112]

One interesting observation of the level of technology adoption among firms under the PCAOB regulatory jurisdiction relates to its adoptions for fully remote inspections during the COVID-19 pandemic period. The PCAOB notes that audit firms responded by providing the PCAOB with documentation via hard copies and laptops and USB drives with required documents and data, but some also used cloud-based services and video chats to comply with inspection requirements.

[111] PCAOB, "Strategic Plan 2020-2024," *https://pcaob-assets.azureedge.net/pcaob-dev/docs/default-source/about/administration/documents/strategic_plans/strategic-plan-2020-2024.pdf?sfvrsn=776073d3_4*

[112] PCAOB, "Changes in Use of Data and Technology in the Conduct of Audits," June 2021, *https://pcaobus.org/oversight/standards/research-standard-setting-projects/changes-use-data-technology-conduct-audits*

7.3 Blockchain Technology: New Opportunities Bring New Risk

The COSO Internal Control – Integrated Framework[113] may provide an approach that can be leveraged to design and implement controls to address the unique risk associated with blockchain. ISACA defines blockchain as a shared transactions ledger that can be accessed by and among multiple parties, using cryptography and peer-to-peer technology to secure data into blocks and store them in an immutable chain of transactions, without any trusted central authority. Although this working definition is helpful, ISACA concurs with the COSO statement that many different types of blockchains exist; there is no singular blockchain.

To address the many blockchain types and the various controls associated with them, an AICPA® white paper published in 2020 provides some examples of how service organizations can use blockchain in systems that provide services to user entities and the risk and control issues presented.[114] The use of blockchain technology by a service organization to provide services to user entities may introduce significant risk and new control issues to the organization. As users of blockchain technology, smart contracts also create potential new risk but can also be an important part of an enterprise risk mitigation tool set. After smart contracts are put in place, they self-execute and are difficult to stop. Therefore, if developed incorrectly or manipulated, the effects could lead to error or potentially significant loss on a magnified scale.

The "Blockchain and Internal Control: The COSO Perspective" white paper provides several examples of how ICFR is likely to change in a blockchain environment, because the underlying processes change dramatically.[115]

- Internal controls related to the control environment change because, in many cases, control no longer rests within the entity.
- The use of a blockchain solution for reconciliation-heavy areas, such as intercompany transactions, may help streamline those processes, make them more efficient and increase visibility for all parties to the transaction.
- Certain types of confirmations may be unnecessary with the ability to re-perform calculations of transactions on the blockchain.
- Blockchains may change the nature of the organization's relationships with vendors and suppliers, for example, how transactions are processed, visibility to pricing, and reporting and transparency of information for returns and rebates.
- There may be no singular external entity that can be held accountable for achieving the control objectives or responsible when there are problems, because a blockchain may not be governed by a singular, centralized management team.
- The demand for SOC reporting in blockchain environments will likely increase. However, without centralized management, there may be no simple or easy way to engage a SOC auditor.
- Some blockchains have their own integrated digital payment or value that exists nowhere else and cannot be tracked any other way. Traditional systems can link into banking or other financial systems; blockchain is sometimes the system itself.
- An important benefit from certain blockchains is the automatic creation and presence of an electronic record of all transactions (i.e., an audit trail). However, just because a transaction is on a blockchain does not necessarily validate the transaction for books and records purposes.
- The work of external and internal auditors may be facilitated by the increased automation of controls and interactions with other emerging technologies (e.g., AI and Internet of Things [IoT]). A blockchain-facilitated

[113] *Op cit* COSO, "Internal Control – Integrated Framework, Executive Summary." Used with permission.

[114] AICPA, "Implications of the Use of Blockchain in SOC for Service Organization Examinations," 2020, *www.aicpa.org/content/dam/aicpa/interestareas/frc/assuranceadvisoryservices/downloadabledocuments/implications-of-blockchain-web.pdf*

[115] Burns, J.; A. Steele; E. Cohen; S. Ramamoorti; "Blockchain and Internal Control: The COSO Perspective," *www.coso.org/Documents/Blockchain-and-Internal-Control-The-COSO-Perspective-Guidance.pdf*

internal control environment may provide a more reliable internal audit environment on which external auditors may be able to better rely.

- More substantive and substantial continuous real-time financial reports are possible and may become routine.

One critical consideration for using blockchain technology for internal controls over financial reporting is the acknowledgment by internal auditors that blockchain is ethereal and continues to evolve. Stability will increase when regulatory and standards organizations catch up and clarify the use cases and governance required for blockchains, digital assets and related technology.[116]

7.4 Audits of ICFR and Cryptoassets

The Financial Accounting Standards Board (FASB), which sets accounting standards for public and private enterprises and nonprofits in the United States, rejected three prior attempts to persuade them to develop accounting standards for cryptoassets, most recently in October 2020. The rationale for rejecting the requests is that investing in cryptocurrencies is not yet widespread among enterprises. FASB launched a new agenda consultation in July 2021 and is expected to weigh in again by early 2022 about whether FASB will consider beginning the years-long process of developing accounting standards for cryptoassets. Because there are no specific binding accounting standards yet, enterprises with cryptoholdings classify them as indefinite-lived intangible assets—similar to trademarks and website domains—following nonbinding guidelines from the AICPA.

The International Financial Reporting Standards Foundation (IFRS) also does not include specific guidance on the accounting for cryptoassets; therefore, industry practice is developing in real time. In June 2019, the IFRS Interpretations Committee concluded that International Accounting Standard 2 (IAS 2*) Inventories* applies to cryptoassets where they are held for sale in the ordinary course of business. If IAS 2 is not applicable, an entity applies IAS 38 *Intangible Assets* to holdings of cryptocurrencies, consistent with the AICPA guidelines.

As a result, auditors are learning by doing and by observing how external auditors step up to meet the SOX and PCAOB AS 2201 requirements when enterprises hold or transact in cryptoassets. The largest public accounting firms are leading the way by establishing accepted practice when addressing these issues at consulting and external audit clients.

In May 2020, the PCAOB highlighted some considerations for auditors addressing audits under PCAOB standards for issuers transacting in or holding cryptoassets.[117] When performing inspections of auditors of some smaller public enterprises, PCAOB staff observed transactions involving cryptoassets that were material to the financial statements. However, the PCAOB does not specifically address any other applications of blockchain, distributed ledger or other technology, in the 2020 document. The information in the PCAOB document is not official guidance but, instead, highlights timely and relevant observations for auditors and audit committees. The document does not establish rules of the PCAOB, nor is it approved by the PCAOB board members.

The PCAOB's first recommendation to external auditors regarding audits of enterprises that transact in or hold cryptoassets is to manage their acceptance and continuance risk by only accepting those engagements for clients with cryptoasset investments and activities that the firm can reasonably expect to be completed with professional competence. The US SEC staff provides information and guidance about digital assets on its website.[118] The

[116] For additional sources of information from regulators and industry organizations outside of the United States, see ACCA Global, "Divided We Fall, Distributed We Stand," 2017, *www.accaglobal.com/gb/en/technical-activities/technical-resources-search/2017/april/divided-we-fall-distributed-we-stand.html*, and ICAEW, "Blockchain and the Future of Accountancy," 20 May 2021, *www.icaew.com/technical/technology/blockchain/blockchain-articles/blockchain-and-the-accounting-perspective*

[117] PCAOB, "Audits Involving Cryptoassets: Information for Auditors and Audit Committees," *Spotlight*, May 2020, *https://pcaobus.org/Documents/Audits-Involving-Cryptoassets-Spotlight.pdf*

[118] See US Securities and Exchange Commission, "Strategic Hub for Innovation and Financial Technology (FinHub)," *www.sec.gov/finhub*. See also Clayton, J.; "Chairman's Testimony on Virtual Currencies: The Roles of the SEC and CFTC," 6 February 2018, *www.sec.gov/news/testimony/testimony-virtual-currencies-oversight-role-us-securities-and-exchange-commission*.

Canadian Public Accountability Board also discusses its findings from its inspections of audits involving cryptoassets.[119]

Audits involving cryptoassets require specialized skill and knowledge, and the performance of engagement quality reviews also requires appropriate levels of knowledge and competence relating to cryptoassets. That specialized skill or knowledge should also include understanding the existing legal and regulatory frameworks for cryptoassets where the enterprise operates or serves customers. Auditors should plan the audits involving cryptoassets that they accept with the requirement for specialized crypto-related knowledge in mind.

Because holdings of cryptoassets are designed to be pseudonymous, audit firms should also consider the risk associated with providing professional services when it may be more difficult for an auditor to recognize when a cryptoasset-related transaction involves fraud or an illegal act. The pseudonymous nature of transactions involving cryptoassets may expose the enterprise to the risk of noncompliance with Know Your Client and anti-money laundering (AML) or AML provisions or create the risk of not identifying the involvement of related parties.

When developing an understanding of the external audit client's risk environment, the auditors should obtain and analyze relevant information about the nature of the enterprise transactions involving cryptoassets. For example, the type of potential misstatements associated with financial statement balances for cryptoassets activity can depend on whether the cryptoassets are stored in the issuer's digital wallet or by a third party.

The external auditor's ability to audit an organization engaged in cryptoasset activities is dependent on, among other things, the use of cryptoassets in the business of the organization, for example, as an investment, as a medium of exchange to effect transactions, held for sale as an input into its own products or services, as an asset that is purchased with a view to its resale in the near future and to generate a profit from changes in the price or via commissions, or as a capital raising tool. IT auditors can support enterprise responses to external audit inquiries by becoming familiar with the relevant internal controls over all the transactions involving cryptoassets that their organization may process in the ordinary course of its business.

These internal controls may include:

- Ensuring completeness of recording cryptoassets and transactions and evaluating controls that make sure an organization accounts for all its cryptocurrency wallets (and the related cryptocurrency that it owns) and all related transactions.
- Understanding controls over the generation and management of private keys (i.e., access passcodes), including the risk of management override of controls over the private keys, which may result in misuse or misappropriation of holdings of cryptoassets by those who control the keys.
- Being able to generate independent substantive audit evidence of the private key and public address pairing, a key element needed to establish ownership of cryptoassets.
- Determining whether a service auditor's report addresses controls at a third party, and whether the controls need to be tested directly by the issuer's auditor to obtain evidence of their effectiveness.
- Understanding controls over the reliability of blockchain information that is audit evidence (e.g., controls that address alterations to the information stored on blockchain), for example, to verify that transactions are authentic and not duplicated. A feature common to all blockchains is that after a transaction is confirmed on the blockchain, it is irreversible. An entity will potentially lose cryptocurrency if it is sent to the wrong address, in error or for fraudulent purposes. IT auditors need the ability to securely interrogate the blockchain to gather corroborating information independently and reliably about blockchain transactions and balances.

[119] See Canadian Public Accountability Board, "Auditing in the Crypto-Asset Sector: Inspections Insights," November 2019, *www.cpab-ccrc.ca/docs/default-source/inspections-reports/2019-crypto-inspections-insights-en.pdf?sfvrsn=9aa5c0d2_20*. See also Chartered Professional Accountants Canada, "Audit Considerations Related to Cryptocurrency Assets and Transactions," 25 September 2021, *www.iasplus.com/en-ca/publications/cpa-canada/audit-considerations-related-to-cryptocurrency-assets-and-transactions*.

- Understanding controls over cryptoasset-related transactions that are recorded outside the blockchain (e.g., information about customer transactions in a trading platform system) and not covered by the same controls as transactions recorded on the blockchain.

The likelihood and magnitude of potential misstatements associated with transactions involving cryptoassets depends on the number of cryptoasset types, the number of customers, the volume of transactions and the nature of record keeping, such as whether customer transactions are recorded outside the blockchain. Organizations that enable transactions in cryptoassets or hold cryptoassets as assets or liabilities create unique new risk that requires new internal controls to mitigate that risk. A 2021 article in the *Journal of Accountancy*®[120] provides some illustrative examples:

- **Valuation**—FASB defines fair value as "the price that would be received to sell an asset or paid to transfer a liability in an orderly transaction between market participants at the measurement date."[121] Recurring high cryptoasset price volatility means market price is not a reliable sign of fair value.
- **Accounting processes and systems**—Existing software is based on foreign currency accounting. A cryptoasset is not currency and using intangible assets as a transaction medium requires new accounting policy, procedure and process establishment and documentation.
- **Knowledge and understanding**—Few people possess the necessary competence and capability regarding cryptoasset accounting to design operational policies, procedures and processes; perform risk assessment and mitigation; and advise senior management and boards of directors so that they can perform proper oversight.

The external auditor, with the support of internal auditors, must obtain a sufficient understanding of internal control over financial reporting for entities that transact or hold cryptoassets, including their information system(s) relevant to financial reporting, to identify the types of potential misstatement, assess the factors that affect the risk of material misstatement and design further audit procedures.

7.5 Impact of Artificial Intelligence

Artificial intelligence uses intelligent machines to work and respond like humans for decision making, problem solving, and activities that require visual perception and speech recognition. AI can transform an organization when used to augment people involvement or as a complete replacement for human interaction with business processes. AI software can be trained to recognize patterns in data or spot anomalies, which is particularly useful when large amounts of transactional data or digital information must be analyzed quickly (e.g., on a blockchain).

However, AI-related risk includes confidence, ethics and marketplace uncertainties:[122]

- **Confidence**—Whether an AI tool provides reliable results
- **Ethics**—Questions about whether using AI is good and right for society, regarding issues of data privacy, fairness, bias and the potential for job loss
- **Marketplace uncertainties**—The effect of a changing regulatory landscape and public or employee opinion on the usefulness of an AI tool

One challenge for internal and external auditors evaluating controls over AI-enabled business processes is that the more powerful the software, the more complex it is. Machine learning models may become so complex that highly trained data scientists will have difficulty understanding precisely how they work. Therefore, organizations and their

[120] Mishler, M.D.; "A take on cryptoasset transactions, investments, and risk," *Journal of Accountancy*®, 1 September 2021, *www.journalofaccountancy.com/issues/2021/sep/cryptoasset-transactions-investments-risk.html*

[121] FASB, "Accounting Standards Update: Fair Value Measurement (Topic 820)," Financial Accounting Series, No. 2011-04, May 2011, *https://asc.fasb.org/imageRoot/00/7534500.pdf*

[122] Ammanath, B.; D.R. Novak; S. Anderson; A. Kulkarni; "Conquering AI risks: Unpacking and alleviating concerns that threaten AI advancement," Deloitte®, 28 October 2020, *www2.deloitte.com/us/en/insights/focus/cognitive-technologies/conquering-ai-risks.html*

auditors will have a harder time justifying the decisions, evaluating the controls, and satisfying regulators and investors that neural networks are producing the correct results and, therefore, the correct financial information.

Another risk for internal and external auditors is increased responsibility for confidential customer information and personally identifiable information (PII), because using AI effectively for audits often requires access to large amounts of confidential data. External auditors may find clients resistant to providing access to high-value data and information. Internal auditors may not have the sufficient tools and protocols in place to protect the data. All auditors must consider the risk and rules associated with data and privacy, and design audit programs that protect sensitive data.

AI is highly vulnerable to cybersecurity incidents. The type of cybersecurity risk that an enterprise may face from an AI implementation depends on the type of enterprise business and, in some cases, where its operations are located.[123] Hackers may use AI to steal sensitive or proprietary data or to manipulate proprietary data or algorithms. AI can also automate the tasks required to commit a cyberattack, or AI code can leave holes that make an enterprise more vulnerable. AI can be used to impersonate authorized users and bypass cyberdefenses. The good news is that AI can also be used to help detect and mitigate these threats.

7.6 Big Data and Data Analytics

Data analytics is growing in use for assessing risk and evaluating controls by management, internal auditors and external auditors. This tool can be very powerful, due to more advanced ERP and business intelligence solutions and an exponential increase in processing power over the last five years. Big data refers to the wide variety of data coming from sources such as IoT, social media and other data sources too large or complex to be processed by traditional applications or manually. Open data are a subset of big data that describe large data sets that are usually structured and produced by government agencies like the SEC. Big data, IoT, AI and blockchain may work together and with internal control processes to become a powerful tool set.

There are four types of data analytics:

- Descriptive analytics uses statistical or judgmental samples to describe what has happened over a given period of time, based on using observation, walkthrough or hard-copy documents. Has cost of sales increased based on higher reported revenue? Has cash increased as accounts receivable days sales outstanding (DSO) has decreased? Descriptive analyses often provide valuable insight into controls and business processes.
- Diagnostic analytics takes advantage of multiple sources of data and assumptions to tell the story of why something happened. Analytics and data extraction tools, such as Audit Command Language (ACL), are run on a one-off basis to address a specific question. Automated and standardized scripts are used for specific reviews. Specialists extract and analyze data to answer complex questions about correlation and causation.
- Predictive analytics gets the closest to AI by using complex data sets that must be cleaned and normalized to attempt to describe what might happen in the near term. Normality is learned and relearned on demand using stylized scenarios, including introduction of false positives and incorporation of new scenarios and variables as required to train the tool. Exceptions in patterns and risk are exposed so that proactive and predictive actions can be taken.
- Prescriptive analytics makes recommendations for optimal decision making to achieve business objectives. IBM® coined the term prescriptive analytics, which uses structured and unstructured data to enable complex decision making based on millions of decision variables, constraints and tradeoffs. Prescriptive analytics not only anticipates what will happen and when it will happen, but also why it will happen. It is the opposite of descriptive analytics, which mines historical data to understand past success or failure.

[123] Ramachandran, K.; "Cybersecurity issues in the AI world: Using AI to address AI-driven cyber attacks," Deloitte, 11 September 2019, *www2.deloitte.com/us/en/pages/technology-media-and-telecommunications/articles/ai-and-cybersecurity-concerns.html*

When an organization is ready for continuous assurance of the enterprise risk management activities, internal auditors can deploy the full suite of automated data analytics with an emphasis on aligning continuous data analysis with the organization strategic goals. The internal audit plan becomes dynamic, able to respond to changes in risk levels.

7.7 Robotic Process Automation

The implementation of robotic process automation processes using digital workers, often referred to as bots is an IT-dependent initiative. Process transformation using RPA requires changes to controls over system access, change management and system development life cycle activities. The development of the bots must be documented to aid in adjusting the system of internal controls. New bots and their configurations must be tested, and management must maintain sufficient documentation for the baseline process to be able to verify if the automated control operates consistently with the underlying program, code and configuration.

Internal and external auditors use the documentation of how the bots work and where the controls are comparable to the policies, procedures and control flowcharts to perform appropriate automated control testing procedures. Distinguishing between human access and bot access to the same applications is critical, and segregation of duties may be challenging.[124]

7.8 Process Mining

Process mining is a technique that can support and tie together many of the latest approaches to data analytics and automation. Process mining discovers the processes and creates the algorithm that allows tools like RPA and AI to automate activities and the monitoring and auditing of those activities. Organizations record and store the event detail from system processes in event logs. Process mining—and its companion task mining, which collects the actions of the people who are making the business processes happen—analyze the chronological data set that describes various processes, such as purchase to pay (P2P), order to cash (O2C) or order management processes. Software tools use the event logs to create a process model, or algorithm, from the observed behavior.

Process mining creates visual representations of the data, which helps internal and external auditors and consultants communicate issues and opportunities inside and outside an organization supporting data-driven decision making. If the algorithm evaluates 100 percent of enterprise transactions, internal auditors can detect potential internal control weaknesses on the entire population rather than just a sample. According to *The CPA Journal*:

> *Under section 404 of the Sarbanes-Oxley Act of 2002 (SOX), it is critical for auditors to evaluate a company's internal control system and identify what can go wrong. Process mining can be a powerful tool to help auditors in performing tests of internal controls. Moreover, the information stored in the event log can also provide audit evidence related to relevant management assertions.*[125]

7.9 Internet of Things

Internet of Things (IoT) refers to the myriad of physical devices all over the world that are connected to the Internet and collecting and sharing data. Security cameras and access devices, environmental controls, and utilities access are all seemingly innocuous ways that enterprises open, close, turn on, turn off and control business and infrastructure that are dependent and exposed to connectivity to the Internet. IoT devices can potentially write to or act on information in a blockchain to assist auditors in their work.

[124] Deloitte, "Financial reporting RPA risks and controls," 2020, *www2.deloitte.com/us/en/pages/audit/articles/financial-reporting-rpa-risks-and-controls.html*

[125] Chiu, T.; H. Brown-Liburd; M. Vasarhelyi; "Performing Tests of Internal Controls Using Process Mining," *The CPA Journal*, July 2019, *www.cpajournal.com/2019/07/10/performing-tests-of-internal-controls-using-process-mining/*

The PCAOB noted in its 2021 Data and Technology Project update[126] that some enterprises are using technology-based tools, such as location cameras and drones, to conduct inventory counts on a remote basis. Those activities became more common due to the necessities of the COVID-19 pandemic period, but the tools were ready and waiting to be used by more organizations. During the COVID-19 pandemic period, the PCAOB observed these tools being used by auditors to facilitate remote performance of annual physical inventory observations or to verify existence of physical assets or business activity at a manufacturing plant (e.g., when the tools are operated by management, internal audit or a third-party vendor, the auditor can perform certain procedures to evaluate the sufficiency of audit evidence produced). This can include assessing vendor qualifications.

7.10 Emerging Technology in Control Assessment

Emerging technology can assist in control management. For example, robotization can automate work processes. Data analysis, potentially aided by AI, can prevent errors from occurring, as a proactive preventive control; detect vulnerabilities, as a detective control; and provide thorough and detailed analyses in the event of a weakness or need to remediate.

Enterprises may also introduce governance, risk and control (GRC) software to monitor and manage their ICFR program. GRC systems organize, document and automate risk and controls evaluations using data collected directly from the ERPs and subsidiary systems in a standard tool with predefined controls. GRC systems and reusable data analytics solutions also enable continuous monitoring within the business processes, which is useful for monitoring and risk assessment purposes.

[126] *Op cit* PCAOB, "Data and Technology Research Project Update"

APPENDIX A

Entity-Level/Activity-Level and IT General Controls for Sarbanes-Oxley

In developing this publication, the IT control objectives and control activities to test were derived using COBIT 2019. Only COBIT 2019 guidance that is considered significant to the exercise of ICFR was selected and tailored for use in this publication.

Entity-Level IT Controls

IT general controls include objectives at the entity level and activity level and are addressed in this publication. However, this publication shows entity-level controls in a questionnaire style and not at a detailed control activity level because of the indirect impact on the financial reporting.

Enterprises should be careful not to simply answer yes or no to the questions. The purpose of the questions is to initiate a dialog that yields examples of how the controls are performed that can be evidenced with documentation or through corroborative inquiry.

Enterprises should add or exclude controls, as appropriate; in this regard, they are encouraged to follow guidance from *COBIT® 2019 Framework: Governance and Management Objectives* and *COBIT® 2019 Design Guide: Designing an Information and Technology Governance Solution.*

Figures A.1 through **A.17** provide considerations for the entity-level assessment of an enterprise IT control environment. Because most enterprises are using the COSO control framework for their internal control program, the figures are structured in the same order as the COSO framework components. The principles are not duplicated in the questionnaires and address points that can be considered when determining whether an entity-level objective has been achieved.

Control Environment

The control environment creates the foundation for effective internal control, establishes the tone at the top and represents the apex of the corporate governance structure. The issues raised in the control environment component apply throughout an IT organization and in setting the framework for the interaction of IT with its stakeholders.

Figure A.1—Control Environment Considerations

Questionnaire	COBIT 2019 Practice Reference	Response/ Evidence
Governance		
1. Are the IT governance systems aligned with the enterprise? Specifically, the ethical use and processing of information and its impact on society, the natural environment, and internal and external stakeholder interests should align with the enterprise direction, goals and objectives.	EDM01.01 APO01.01 APO02.01	
IT Strategic Planning		
2. Has management prepared strategic plans for IT that align business objectives with IT strategies? Does the planning approach include mechanisms to solicit input from relevant internal and external stakeholders affected by the IT strategic plans?	APO02.01 APO02.05	

Figure A.1—Control Environment Considerations *(cont.)*		
Questionnaire	**COBIT 2019 Practice Reference**	**Response/ Evidence**
3. Does the IT organization communicate its IT plans to business stakeholders, process owners and other relevant parties across the enterprise?	EDM05.02 APO02.06	
4. Does IT management communicate its activities, challenges and risk on a regular basis with the CEO and CFO? Is this information also shared with the board of directors?	EDM01.02 APO02.06	
5. Does the IT organization monitor its progress against the strategic plan (gap analysis) and react accordingly to meet established objectives? Does IT analyze and report performance periodically against targets, using a method that provides a succinct all-around view that fits within the enterprise monitoring system? Have target digital capabilities been defined?	EDM05.03 APO02.02 APO02.03 APO02.04 APO02.05 MEA01.04	
IT Processes, Organization and Relationships		
6. Do IT managers have adequate knowledge and experience to fulfill their responsibilities?	APO07.03	
7. Have relevant systems and data been inventoried and their owners identified?	APO01.07	
8. Are roles and responsibilities of the IT organization defined, documented and understood?	EDM01.02 APO01.05 APO07.01	
9. Does the enterprise plan and track the usage of IT and business human resources?	APO07.05	
10. Have data integrity ownership and responsibilities been communicated to appropriate data/business owners and have they accepted these responsibilities?	APO01.05 APO01.07 APO14.01	
11. Have key IT personnel been identified to minimize reliance on a single individual performing a critical job function?	APO07.02	
12. Has IT management implemented a division of roles and responsibilities (segregation of duties [SoD]) that reasonably prevents a single individual from subverting a critical process?	APO01.05	
Manage the Enablers and Communication Objectives and Direction of the Enterprise		
13. Has the IT organization adopted and promoted the enterprise culture of integrity management, including ethics, business practices and human resources evaluations?	EDM01.02 APO01.02	
Educate and Train Users		
14. Does IT management provide education and ongoing training programs that include system security practices, confidentiality standards and security responsibilities of all staff?	APO07.03	

Information and Communication

COSO states that information is needed at all levels of an enterprise to run the business and achieve the enterprise control objectives. However, the identification, management and communication of important information represent an ever-increasing challenge to the IT department. The determination of this information is required to achieve control objectives.

The communication of this information in a form and time frame that allow people to carry out their duties supports the other four components of the COSO framework.

Figure A.2—Information and Communication Considerations

Questionnaire	COBIT 2019 Practice Reference	Response/ Evidence
Communicate Management Aims and Directions		
15. Does IT management periodically review its policies, procedures and standards to reflect changing business conditions?	APO01.02 APO01.09	
16. Does IT management have a process in place to assess compliance with its policies, procedures and standards?	APO01.09 MEA02	
17. Does IT management understand its roles and responsibilities related to the Sarbanes-Oxley Act?	MEA03.01 MEA03.02	

Risk Assessment

Risk assessment involves the identification and analysis by management of significant risk factors to achieve predetermined objectives, which form the basis for determining control activities. It is likely that internal control risk could be more pervasive in the IT organization than in other areas of the enterprise. Risk assessment may occur at the entity level (for the overall enterprise) or at the activity level (for a specific process or business unit).

Figure A.3—Risk Assessment Considerations

Questionnaire	COBIT 2019 Practice Reference	Response/ Evidence
Assess and Manage IT Risk		
18. Does the IT organization have an entity- and activity-level risk assessment framework that it uses periodically to assess information risk to achieve financial reporting objectives? Does it consider the probability and likelihood of threats?	EDM03.01 EDM03.02 EDM03.03	
19. Does the IT organization risk assessment framework measure the impact of risk according to qualitative and quantitative criteria, using inputs from different areas including, but not limited to, management brainstorming, strategic planning, past audits and other assessments?	APO12.01 APO12.02 APO12.03 APO12.04	
20. Where risk factors are considered acceptable, is there formal documentation and acceptance of residual risk with related offsets, including adequate insurance coverage, contractually negotiated liabilities and self-insurance? Where risk factors have not been accepted, does management have an action plan to implement a risk response?	APO12.05 APO12.06	

Monitoring Activities

Monitoring, which covers the oversight of internal control by management through continuous and point-in-time assessment processes, is becoming increasingly important to IT management.

Figure A.4—Monitoring Considerations		
Questionnaire	COBIT 2019 Practice Reference	Response/ Evidence
Manage Quality		
21. Is documentation created and maintained for significant IT processes, controls and activities?	APO11.01 APO11.03	
22. Does a quality plan exist for significant IT functions (e.g., system development and deployment) and does it provide a consistent approach to address both general and project-specific quality assurance activities?	APO11.02 APO11.04 APO11.05 BAI03.06 BAI11.05	
Monitor and Evaluate Performance		
23. Has IT management established appropriate metrics to effectively manage the day-to-day activities of the IT department?	MEA01.01 MEA01.02 MEA01.03	
24. Does IT management monitor IT delivery of services to identify shortfalls and does IT respond with actionable plans to improve?	MEA01.04 MEA01.05	
Monitor and Evaluate Internal Control		
25. Does IT management obtain independent reviews of its operations, including policies, procedures, overall IT systems and processes, and does IT management assess adherence to those policies and procedures?	EDM01.03 MEA02.01 MEA02.02 MEA02.04 MEA04.01	
26. Does the enterprise have an IT internal audit function that is responsible for reviewing IT activities and controls, including general and application controls? Is there a follow-up process for residual actions? Is there a mechanism to allow monitoring of internal control of third-party service providers?	APO10.05 DSS01.02 MEA02.01 MEA04.01 MEA04.02 MEA04.04 MEA04.05 MEA04.06 MEA04.07 MEA04.08 MEA04.09	

Activity-Level IT Controls

Activity-level IT controls provide information to enable management reporting to regulators, investors and stakeholders in a life cycle of collecting complete and accurate information and reporting it on a timely basis. As one might expect, this life cycle is highly dependent on information systems, such as applications, databases and other tools that are used to enhance the efficiency and effectiveness of data processing.

The balance of this appendix provides guidance on IT controls that are designed to support financial reporting objectives. These controls are not intended to be an exhaustive list nor are they completely representative of what may be considered by the external auditor. However, they do provide a starting point as enterprises determine which

IT controls are necessary for their environment. Consideration should also be given to IT controls that may not be included in the following tables, but which an enterprise considers relevant to its specific environment.

In **figures A.5** through **A.17**, some controls are identified with a star (✯) indicating that the control is a key control. The key internal controls are those that are applicable to financial statement assertions. They include activities that prevent or detect and correct a significant misstatement in financial reporting or other required disclosures, including those over recording amounts into the general ledger and recording journal entries (standard, nonstandard and consolidation). The key controls may be manual or automated, and preventive or detective in nature. This definition is applied to the controls in **figures A.5** through **A.17** to identify those that are commonly required to comply with Sarbanes-Oxley. Note that in the titles of **figures A.5** through **A.17**, COBIT 2019 governance and management objectives are listed in parentheses.

This guidance is not intended to be exhaustive. Professional judgment, as always, needs to be applied when determining the necessary controls that should be included in the compliance program, including some which may not be highlighted as key controls in this publication.

Managed Requirements Definition (BAI02, BAI04)

Control Guidance

Control objective—Controls provide reasonable assurance that business functional and technical requirements are maintained with a feasibility study that considers alternative solutions, enterprise risk and approvals.

Rationale—The process of building, acquiring and developing business processes, applications, infrastructure, data and services includes the definition of business requirements in the design, development and acquisition of systems that support the achievement of business objectives. Deficiencies in this area may have a significant impact on financial reporting and disclosure. For instance, without sufficient controls over application interfaces, financial information may not be complete or accurate.

Figure A.5—Managed Requirements Definition (BAI02, BAI04)

Control Objectives	Control Activities to Test	COBIT 2019 References
The enterprise has a system that defines and maintains business functional and technical requirements that are endorsed by all stakeholders. ✯	Confirm, elicit and analyze that all stakeholder requirements, including relevant acceptance criteria, are considered, captured, prioritized and recorded in a way that is understandable to the stakeholders, business sponsors and technical implementation personnel. Verify that data and information control requirements and automated processes, where appropriate, that address information risk to comply with laws, regulations and commercial contracts, are included. Verify that requirements meet enterprise policies and standards, enterprise architecture, in-house and outsourced business and IT processes, security requirements and regulatory requirements. Verify that an assessment of the current availability, system performance and capacity has been undertaken. Verify that a plan for new or changed service requirements based on system performance, availability and capacity exists.	BAI02.01 BAI04.01 BAI04.03

Figure A.5—Managed Requirements Definition (BAI02, BAI04) *(cont.)*		
Control Objectives	**Control Activities to Test**	**COBIT 2019 References**
The enterprise has a system that performs a feasibility study, including the formulation of alternative solutions.	Obtain a copy of a recent feasibility study. Identify required actions for an acquisition or development solution based on the enterprise architecture, taking into consideration scope and budget constraints. Ensure that the study is translated into a high-level acquisition/development plan.	BAI02.02
The enterprise has a system for identifying, documenting, prioritizing and mitigating technical and information processing-related risk associated with the enterprise requirements and proposed solutions.	Obtain a copy of a risk register that demonstrates stakeholder involvement, including business sponsor and process owner. Ensure appropriate risk response is determined to requirements risk. Ensure that the business sponsor or product owner makes the final decision with respect to choice of solution, acquisition approach and high-level design according to the business case. Verify that a business impact analysis has been undertaken once a system performance capacity baseline has been performed.	BAI02.03 BAI02.04 BAI04.02

Managed Solutions Identification and Build (BAI03, BAI04)

Control Guidance

Control objective—Controls provide reasonable assurance that solutions are identified and maintained in line with enterprise requirements covering design, development, and procurement/sourcing and partnering with suppliers/vendors. In addition, they include configuration management, test preparation, the maintenance of business processes, applications, infrastructure, information/data and services so that they provide the appropriate platforms to support financial reporting applications.

Rationale—The process of building, acquiring and implementing software applications and technology infrastructure includes the design, acquisition/building and deployment of systems that support the achievement of business objectives. This process includes not only major changes to existing systems, but the infrastructure components, including servers, networks and databases, that are critical for secure and reliable information processing. Without adequate applications and infrastructure, there is an increased risk that financial reporting applications will not be able to pass data between applications, that financial reporting applications will not operate and that critical infrastructure failures will not be detected in a timely manner.

Figure A.6—Managed Solutions Identification and Build (BAI03, BAI04)		
Control Objectives	**Control Activities to Test**	**COBIT 2019 References**
The enterprise has a development technique that allows for high-level and detailed designs that align with the enterprise architecture and IT strategy. ✯	Select a sample of approved high-level design specifications and verify that they are consistent with the enterprise design standards, enterprise architecture, security/privacy plan and relevant laws, regulations and contracts. Ensure that they are appropriately approved and meet the proposed solutions. Select a sample of approved detailed design specifications and verify that: • The design explains the application processing steps (e.g., specification of transaction types), business processing rules, automated controls, data definitions/business objects, use cases, external interfaces, design constraints and other requirements (e.g., licensing, legal and standards). • The design includes audit transactions to identify root causes of processing errors.	BAI03.01 BAI03.02 BAI04.03

Figure A.6—Managed Solutions Identification and Build (BAI03, BAI04) *(cont.)*		
Control Objectives	**Control Activities to Test**	**COBIT 2019 References**
The enterprise has a process for the procurement or development of solution components that includes all control requirements in the business process, supporting IT applications and infrastructure services. ✯	Select and examine a sample of acquisition plans, which should include future capacity additions, transition costs, risk and upgrades over the project life cycle. Review change requests, performance and quality reviews, ensuring active participation of all impacted stakeholders. Review configuration requirements of application software.	BAI03.03 BAI03.04 BAI03.05
Documented procedures exist for the preparation of solution testing, taking into consideration quality assurance (QA) plans that are aligned to the enterprise quality management system (QMS).	Review a sample of test plans and verify that they cater to a test environment that supports the full scope of the solution. Identify test logs and check that testing errors are appropriately classified as minor, significant or critical, based on the risk assessment carried out in the requirements and solution building phases.	BAI03.06 BAI03.07 BAI03.08
The enterprise has a system of requirements for change management throughout the project life cycle. ✯	Select a sample of change requests and confirm whether they maintain the integrity of integration and configuration of the solution components. Assess the impact of any major solution upgrade and classify it according to agreed-on objective criteria based on the outcome of the risk analysis.	BAI03.09 BAI04.03
The enterprise has a plan for the ongoing maintenance of the solutions developed and tested. This includes periodic reviews against business needs and operational requirements. ✯	Select a sample of solutions maintenance plans and determine that they include periodic reviews against business needs and operational requirements, such as patch management, upgrade strategies, risk, privacy, vulnerabilities assessment and security requirements. Ensure that, in the event of major changes to existing solutions due to maintenance activity that results in significant change in current designs, functionality and/or business processes, the organization follows the development process used for new systems and for maintenance updates, and that the change management process is followed.	BAI03.10
The enterprise has a process for defining new and changed IT services and service levels. ✯	Check for documentation of service levels and the definition of new and changed IT services. Ensure that service levels for outsourced vendors are defined, agreed on and monitored. Ensure that they are complete, including such items as service times, availability, security, continuity compliance and usability. Check for the existence of a service portfolio or catalog.	BAI03.11 BAI04.03
The enterprise has a process for designing solutions based on a defined development methodology. ✯	Verify that an approved development methodology is followed to design, develop and implement solutions in accordance with the overall strategy and requirements.	BAI03.12

Managed Compliance with Policies and Procedures (APO01, DSS01)

Control Guidance

Control objective—Controls provide reasonable assurance that a process has been put in place to maintain compliance with, and performance measurement of, policies and procedures and to ensure that they enforce the consequences of noncompliance or inadequate performance.

Rationale—Policies and procedures include the methodology and the process for building, acquiring, implementing and maintaining applications, infrastructure and required procedural documentation. For some enterprises, the policies and procedures include service level agreements (SLAs), operational practices and training materials. Policies and procedures support the enterprise commitment to perform business process activities in a consistent and objective manner.

Figure A.7—Managed Compliance with Policies and Procedures (APO01, DSS01)

Control Objectives	Control Activities to Test	COBIT 2019 References
The enterprise has policies and procedures in place that are periodically reviewed, updated and approved by management. These include, but are not limited to, application and infrastructure development standards, security policy, data storage and output, and IT operations management. ☆	Confirm that the enterprise has policies and procedures in place and, when they are changed, determine whether management approves those changes. Select a sample of these policies and procedures and consider whether they were complied with.	APO01.09 DSS01.01

Managed IT Changes (BAI06)

Control Guidance

Control objective—Controls provide reasonable assurance that system changes of financial reporting significance are authorized and appropriately tested before being moved to production.

Rationale—Managing changes addresses how an enterprise modifies system functionality to help the business meet its financial reporting objectives. Deficiencies in this area can significantly impact financial reporting. For instance, changes to the programs that allocate financial data to accounts require appropriate approvals and testing prior to the change so that proper classification and reporting integrity are maintained.

Figure A.8—Managed IT Changes (BAI06)

Control Objectives	Control Activities to Test	COBIT 2019 References
Requests for program changes, system changes and maintenance (including changes to system software) are standardized, logged, evaluated, prioritized and approved. ☆	Determine that a documented change management process exists and is maintained to reflect the current processes. Consider whether change management procedures exist for all changes to the production environment, including program changes, system maintenance and infrastructure changes. Consider whether change requests are properly initiated, approved and tracked. Review the change request log and select a sample of changes made to applications/systems to determine whether they were adequately tested and approved before being placed into a production environment. Evaluate procedures designed to determine that only authorized/approved changes are moved to production.	BAI06.01

Figure A.8—Managed IT Changes (BAI06) *(cont.)*		
Control Objectives	**Control Activities to Test**	**COBIT 2019 References**
Emergency change requests are documented and subject to formal change management procedures. ★	Determine whether a process exists to control and supervise emergency changes. Determine whether an audit trail exists of all emergency activity and verify that it is independently reviewed. Determine if the procedures require that emergency changes be supported by appropriate documentation. Establish that back-out procedures are developed for emergency changes. Evaluate procedures ensuring that all emergency changes are tested and subject to standard approval procedures after they have been made. Review a sample of changes that are recorded as "emergency" changes, and determine whether they contain the needed approval and the needed access was terminated after a set period of time. Establish that the sample of changes was well documented.	BAI06.02
The enterprise maintains a tracking and reporting system to document rejected changes and to communicate the status of approved and in-process and closed changes. ★	Confirm that a reporting process is in place, with a categorization of change requests (e.g., approved, rejected, in process, not yet initiated and closed). Confirm that an appropriate retention period is defined for change documentation and pre- and post-change system and user documentation.	BAI06.03 BAI06.04
IT management implements system software that does not jeopardize the security of the data and programs being stored on the system. ★	Determine that a risk assessment of the potential impact of changes to system software is performed. Review procedures to test changes to system software in a development environment before they are applied to production. Verify that back-out procedures exist.	BAI06.01

Managed IT Change Acceptance and Transitioning (BAI07)

Control Guidance

Control objective—Controls provide reasonable assurance that the systems are appropriately tested and validated prior to being placed into production processes and associated controls operate as intended and support financial reporting requirements.

Rationale—Installation testing and validating relate to the migration of new systems into production. Before such systems are installed, appropriate testing and validation should be performed to determine whether the systems are operating as designed. Without adequate testing, systems may not function as intended and may provide invalid information, which could result in unreliable financial information and reports.

Figure A.9—Managed IT Change Acceptance and Transitioning (BAI07)		
Control Objectives	**Control Activities to Test**	**COBIT 2019 References**
An implementation plan is established that covers system and data conversion, acceptance testing criteria, communication, training, release preparation, promotion to production, early production support and postimplementation reviews.	Select a sample of system development projects and significant system upgrades. Determine whether an implementation plan was followed. Determine whether a formal testing strategy was carried out. Consider whether the plan considered assessment and mitigation of implementation risk. Consider also the completeness and accuracy of system interfaces that are necessary or essential to promote code or configuration changes to production.	BAI07.01
A business process, system and data conversion plan is established that covers IT service data and infrastructure migration as part of the enterprise development methods, including audit trails and a recovery plan, if migration fails.	Obtain a sample of system development projects and system upgrades that are significant for financial reporting. Determine whether a migration plan was prepared and that it included, e.g., hardware, networks, operating systems, software, transaction data, master files, backups and archives, system interfaces, business procedures and system documentation. For cases where the data conversion required changes in data values, determine that changes are documented and approval from business process data owners is obtained. Verify whether the data conversion was verified by comparing to the original data before conversion.	BAI07.02
An acceptance test plan and test environment are established that define roles and responsibilities, taking into consideration IT operations environment, security, internal controls, operating practices and privacy requirements. ☆	Obtain a sample of system development projects and system upgrades that are significant for financial reporting. Ensure that the test plan identifies necessary resources to execute testing and evaluate results. Confirm that all test plans were approved by stakeholders, including business process owners and IT. Ensure that the test plan identifies testing phases appropriate to the operational requirements and environment. Examples of such testing phases include unit test, system test, integration test, user acceptance test, performance test, stress test, data conversion test, security test, privacy test, operational readiness test, and backup and recovery tests. Ensure that the appropriate level of training has been considered in the plan and the way the training is extended to users on new and upgraded systems is effective. Ensure that the test plan reflects a risk assessment and addresses, if necessary, the need for internal or external accreditation of outcomes (e.g., financial regulatory requirements). Ensure sensitive test data and results are protected against disclosure, including access, retention, storage and destruction.	BAI07.03 BAI07.04

Figure A.9—Managed IT Change Acceptance and Transitioning (BAI07) *(cont.)*		
Control Objectives	**Control Activities to Test**	**COBIT 2019 References**
Acceptance testing is performed and the accepted solutions are promoted to production or software upgrade releases are managed in accordance with the test plans. In some cases, parallel testing or a pilot implementation is undertaken prior to migration. ★	Obtain a sample of system development projects and system upgrades that are significant for financial reporting. Ensure that version controls have been maintained over the changes/upgrades and that access to source code and media libraries is restricted. Review error logs to verify that those errors have been remediated and accepted. Review tests of security requirements, if applicable, taking into consideration security incidents since construction of the test plan. Verify that all media libraries have been updated promptly and that all relevant business process and system, configuration and contingency documentation has been promptly updated. Ensure that approval is obtained from the users/functional personnel on the successful migration of data.	BAI07.05 BAI07.06
The enterprise provides early production support to help stabilize the new solution and conducts a postimplementation review to confirm outcomes and results.	Confirm that additional resources are provided to end users as required and there is a stable operational environment. Confirm by looking at the conversation and support plan. Consult with business process owners and IT technical management when looking at the achievement of requirements and benefits. Consider postimplementation reviews arising outside the business or project, e.g., internal audit or enterprise risk management (ERM) compliance reviews.	BAI07.07 BAI07.08

Managed Service Agreements (APO09)

Control Guidance

Control objective—Controls provide reasonable assurance that service levels are defined and managed in a manner that satisfies financial reporting system requirements and provides a common understanding of performance levels by which the quality of services will be measured.

Rationale—The process of defining and managing service levels addresses how an enterprise meets the functional and operational expectations of its users and, ultimately, the objectives of the business. Roles and responsibilities are defined and an accountability and measurement model is used to determine whether services are delivered as required. Deficiencies in this area could significantly impact financial reporting and disclosure of an enterprise. For instance, if systems are poorly managed or system functionality is not delivered as required, financial information may not be processed as intended.

Figure A.10—Managed Service Agreements (APO09)		
Control Objectives	**Control Activities to Test**	**COBIT 2019 References**
Service levels are defined and managed to support financial reporting system requirements.	Obtain a sample of SLAs and review their content for clearly defined service descriptions and expectations of users. Discuss with members of the enterprise responsible for service level management to determine whether service levels are actively managed. Obtain and test evidence that service levels are being actively managed in accordance with SLAs. Discuss with users whether financial reporting systems are being supported and delivered in accordance with their expectations and SLAs.	APO09.02 APO09.03 APO09.05

Figure A.10—Managed Service Agreements (APO09) *(cont.)*		
Control Objectives	**Control Activities to Test**	**COBIT 2019 References**
A framework is defined to establish appropriate performance indicators to manage SLAs, both internally and externally.	Obtain service level performance reports and confirm that they include key performance indicators (KPIs). Review the performance results and performance issues and assess how service level managers are addressing these issues.	APO09.01 APO09.03 APO09.04

Managed Vendors and Third-Party Services (APO10, DSS01, MEA02)

Control Guidance

Control objective—Controls provide reasonable assurance that suppliers and third-party services are secure, accurate and available; support processing integrity; and are defined appropriately in performance contracts.

Rationale—Managing suppliers and third-party services includes the use of outsourced service providers to support financial applications and related systems. Deficiencies in this area could significantly impact financial reporting and disclosure of an entity. For instance, insufficient controls over processing accuracy by a third-party service provider may result in inaccurate financial results.

Figure A.11—Managed Vendors and Third-party Services (APO10, DSS01, MEA02)		
Control Objectives	**Control Activities to Test**	**COBIT 2019 References**
A designated individual is responsible for regular monitoring and reporting on the achievement of the third-party service level performance criteria.	Determine whether the management of third-party services has been assigned to appropriate individuals. Verify that a formal communication and review process exists, which includes supplier interactions and schedules.	APO10.03
Selection of vendors for outsourced services is performed in accordance with the enterprise vendor management policy and process. ✯	Verify that the enterprise has a standard or policy that contains an evaluation process that includes criteria relating to supplier type, significance, and criticality of contracts enabling the focus on preferred and important suppliers. Assess whether these criteria include consideration of the third party's financial stability, skill and knowledge of the systems under management, and controls over security and processing integrity. Review requests for information (RFIs) and requests for proposals (RFPs) to ensure that they clearly define requirements and award criteria and the decision process. Verify that the evaluation system is documented.	APO10.01 APO10.02
Third-party service contracts address the risk, security controls and procedures for information systems and networks in the contract between the parties. ✯	Select a sample of third-party service contracts and determine whether they include controls to support security and processing integrity in accordance with the enterprise policies and procedures.	APO10.04

Figure A.11—Managed Vendors and Third-party Services (APO10, DSS01, MEA02) *(cont.)*

Control Objectives	Control Activities to Test	COBIT 2019 References
Procedures exist and are followed that include requirements that, for third-party services, a formal contract be defined and agreed to before work is initiated, including definition of internal control requirements and acceptance of the enterprise policies and procedures. ✯	Review a sample of contracts and determine whether: • There is a definition of services to be performed. • The responsibilities for the controls over financial reporting systems have been adequately defined. • The third party has accepted compliance with the enterprise policies and procedures, e.g., security policies and procedures. • The contracts were reviewed and signed by appropriate parties before work commenced. • The controls over financial reporting systems and subsystems described in the contract agree with those required by the enterprise. Review gaps, if any, and consider further analysis to determine the impact on financial reporting.	APO10.03 DSS01.02
A regular review of security and processing integrity is performed by third-party service providers (e.g., SSAE 18 SOC® 1 reporting). ✯	Inquire whether third-party service providers perform independent reviews of security and processing integrity (e.g., a service auditor report). Obtain a sample of the most recent review and determine whether there are any control deficiencies that would impact financial reporting.	APO10.05 DSS01.02 MEA02.01

Managed Systems Security (APO13, DSS02, DSS05, DSS06)

Control Guidance

Control objective—Controls provide reasonable assurance that financial reporting systems and subsystems are appropriately secured to prevent unauthorized use, disclosure, modification, damage or loss of data.

Rationale—Managing systems security includes both physical and logical controls that prevent unauthorized access. These controls typically support authorization, authentication, nonrepudiation, data classification and security monitoring. Deficiencies in this area could significantly impact financial reporting. For instance, insufficient controls over transaction authorization may result in inaccurate financial reporting.

Figure A.12—Ensure Systems Security (APO13, DSS02, DSS05, DSS06)

Control Objectives	Control Activities to Test	COBIT 2019 References
An information security management system plan and policy exist and have been approved by an appropriate level of executive management. ✯	Obtain a copy of the enterprise information security management system (ISMS) and security policy and evaluate their effectiveness. Points to be taken into consideration include: • Are information security (IS) roles and responsibilities defined and communicated? • Is there an overall statement of the importance of security to the enterprise? • Have specific policy objectives been defined? • Have employee and contractor security responsibilities been addressed? • Has the policy been approved by an appropriate level of senior management to demonstrate management's commitment to security? • Is there a process to communicate the policy to all levels of management, employees, contractors, vendors and third parties? • Have all regulatory requirements been considered?	APO13.01 APO13.02
A framework of security standards and a risk treatment plan have been developed that support the objectives of the security policy.	Obtain a copy of the security standards and risk plan. Determine whether the standards framework effectively meets the objectives of the security policy. Consider whether the following topics, which are often addressed by security standards, have been appropriately covered: • Security organization • Roles and responsibilities • Physical and environmental security • Operating system security • Network security • Application security • Database security Determine whether there are processes in place to communicate and maintain these standards.	APO13.01 APO13.02
An IT security and privacy plan exists that is aligned with overall IT strategic plans.	Obtain a copy of security and privacy plans or strategies for financial reporting systems and subsystems and assess their adequacy in relation to the overall company plan.	APO13.02
The IT security plan is updated to reflect changes in the IT environment as well as security requirements of specific systems.	Confirm that the security plan reflects the unique security requirements of financial reporting systems and subsystems.	APO13.03
Procedures exist and are followed to authenticate all users of the system (both internal and external) to support the existence of transactions. ✯	Assess the authentication mechanisms used to validate user credentials for financial reporting systems and subsystems and validate that user sessions time out after a predetermined period of time. Validate that no shared user profiles (including administrative profiles) are used.	DSS05.04 DSS06.03

Figure A.12—Ensure Systems Security (APO13, DSS02, DSS05, DSS06) *(cont.)*		
Control Objectives	**Control Activities to Test**	**COBIT 2019 References**
Procedures exist and are followed to maintain the effectiveness of authentication and access mechanisms (e.g., regular password changes). ✯	Review security practices to confirm that authentication controls (passwords, IDs, two-factor, etc.) are used appropriately and are subject to common confidentiality requirements (IDs and passwords not shared, alphanumeric passwords used, etc.). Validate the configuration settings to ensure adherence to password policies.	DSS05.04
Procedures exist and are followed relating to timely action for requesting, establishing, issuing, suspending and closing user accounts. (Include procedures for authenticating transactions originating outside the enterprise, including contractors, vendors and third parties.) ✯	Confirm that procedures for the registration, change and deletion of users from financial reporting systems and subsystems on a timely basis exist and are followed. Ensure that all regulatory requirements have been considered. Select a sample of new users and determine whether management approved their access and the access granted agrees with the access privileges that were approved. Select a sample of terminated employees and determine whether their access has been removed, and the removal was done in a timely manner. Select a sample of privileged and current users and review their access for appropriateness based on their job functions.	DSS05.04
A control process exists and is followed to periodically review and confirm access rights. ✯	Inquire whether access controls for financial reporting systems and subsystems are reviewed by management on a periodic basis. Assess the adequacy of how exceptions are reexamined and whether the follow-up occurs in a timely manner.	DSS05.04
Where appropriate, controls exist so that neither party can deny transactions and controls are implemented to provide nonrepudiation of origin or receipt, proof of submission, and receipt of transactions.	Determine how the enterprise establishes accountability for transaction initiation and approval. Test the use of accountability controls by observing a user attempting to enter an unauthorized transaction. Obtain a sample of transactions and identify evidence of the accountability or origination of each. Ensure that the integrity and validity of data are maintained throughout the data's processing life cycle: the data are complete, accurate, valid and authorized.	DSS05.06 DSS06.01 DSS06.02 DSS06.03 DSS06.04 DSS06.05
Appropriate controls, including firewalls, intrusion detection and vulnerability assessments, exist and are used to prevent unauthorized access via public networks.	Determine the sufficiency and appropriateness of perimeter security controls, including firewalls and intrusion detection systems (IDSs). Inquire whether management has performed an independent assessment of controls within the past year (e.g., ethical hacking, social engineering). Obtain a copy of this assessment and review the results, including the appropriateness of follow-up on identified weaknesses. Inquire whether periodic penetration testing is conducted to determine the adequacy of network protection. Determine whether antivirus systems are used to protect the integrity and security of financial reporting systems and subsystems. Where appropriate, determine whether encryption techniques are used to support the confidentiality of financial information sent from one system to another.	DSS05.01 DSS05.02 DSS05.03

Figure A.12—Ensure Systems Security (APO13, DSS02, DSS05, DSS06) *(cont.)*		
Control Objectives	**Control Activities to Test**	**COBIT 2019 References**
IT security administration monitors and logs security activity at the operating system, application and database levels, and identified security violations are reported to senior management. ✯	Inquire whether a security office exists to monitor for security vulnerabilities at the application and database levels and related threat events. Assess the nature and extent of such events over the past year and discuss with management how it has responded with controls to prevent unauthorized access or manipulation of financial systems and subsystems. Validate that attempts to gain unauthorized access to financial reporting systems and subsystems are logged and followed up on a timely basis.	DSS02.01 DSS05.07
Controls relating to appropriate segregation of duties over requesting and granting access to systems and data exist and are followed. ✯	Review the process to request and grant access to systems and data and confirm that the same person does not perform these functions.	DSS05.04 DSS06.03
Access to facilities is restricted to authorized personnel and requires appropriate identification and authentication.	Obtain policies and procedures as they relate to facility security and key and card reader access, and determine whether those procedures account for proper identification and authentication. Observe the in-and-out traffic to the enterprise's facilities to establish that proper access is controlled. Select a sample of users and determine whether their access is appropriate based on their job responsibilities.	DSS05.05

Managed Configuration (BAI10)

Control Guidance

Control objective—Controls provide reasonable assurance that IT components, as they relate to security and processing, are well protected, would prevent any unauthorized changes, and assist in the verification and recording of the current configuration.

Rationale—Configuration management provides visibility and control of the performance of software applications and infrastructure over its life cycle. It verifies that a system performs as intended and is identified and documented in sufficient detail to support its projected life cycle. Ineffective configuration controls can lead to security exposures that may permit unauthorized access to systems and data and impact financial reporting. An additional potential risk is corruption to data integrity caused by poor control of the configuration when making system changes or by the introduction of unauthorized system components.

Figure A.13—Managed Configuration (BAI10)		
Control Objectives	**Control Activities to Test**	**COBIT 2019 References**
The enterprise has established and maintains a configuration model that includes all services, assets and infrastructure, how they are recorded, and the relationships among them.	Determine whether such a model exists and includes configuration item (CI) types, attributes and their relationships.	BAI10.01

Figure A.13—Managed Configuration (BAI10) *(cont.)*		
Control Objectives	**Control Activities to Test**	**COBIT 2019 References**
The enterprise has a repository system that caters to the controlled configuration baselines.	Determine whether a repository exists and is populated with all identifiable and classified CIs. Review examples of baselining to see whether there is agreement on and approval of the configuration of services, applications and infrastructure.	BAI10.02
There is a process for maintaining and controlling CIs that deals with the appropriate changes. ✯	Conduct an evaluation of the frequency and timeliness of management's review of configuration records. Confirm that all changes are authorized and the repository updated.	BAI10.03
The enterprise has a reporting process for producing regular status and configuration reports.	Confirm that status reports include changes to CIs and these are matched to approval requests. Report unauthorized changes to management.	BAI10.04

Managed Service Requests and Incidents, Problems (DSS02, DSS03)

Control Guidance

Control objective—Controls provide reasonable assurance that any problems and/or incidents are properly responded to, recorded, resolved or investigated for proper resolution.

Rationale—The process of managing problems and incidents addresses how an enterprise identifies, documents and responds to events that fall outside normal operations. Deficiencies in this area could significantly impact financial reporting.

Figure A.14—Managed Service Requests and Incidents, Problems (DSS02, DSS03)		
Control Objectives	**Control Activities to Test**	**COBIT 2019 References**
IT management has defined and implemented an incident and problem management system such that data integrity and access control incidents are recorded, analyzed, resolved in a timely manner and reported to management. ✯	Determine whether an incident management system exists and how it is being used. Review how management has documented how the system is to be used. Review a sample of incident reports, to consider whether the issues were addressed (recorded, analyzed and resolved) in a timely manner. Review a sample of incidents to consider whether the incidents are properly classified and the incident priority is assigned based on the incident impact and urgency. Determine whether incident escalation rules and procedures exist, especially for major incidents and security incidents.	DSS02.01 DSS02.02 DSS02.03 DSS02.04 DSS02.05 DSS02.06
The problem management system provides for adequate audit trail facilities, which allow tracing from problem or incident to underlying cause.	Determine whether the enterprise procedures include audit trail facilities—tracking of the problems or incidents. Review a sample of problems recorded on the problem management system to consider whether a proper audit trail exists and is used.	DSS03.01 DSS03.02 DSS03.03 DSS03.04 DSS03.05
An incident and problem tracking and reporting system exists that includes a status and escalation procedures.	Review a sample of periodic status reports. Check for frequency and whether an analysis of trends and patterns of recurring issues exists or there are SLA breaches.	DSS02.07

Figure A.14—Managed Service Requests and Incidents, Problems (DSS02, DSS03) *(cont.)*		
Control Objectives	**Control Activities to Test**	**COBIT 2019 References**
IT management has defined and implemented a service requests management system such that all service requests are verified, approved and fulfilled in a timely manner and reported to management. ✯	Determine whether a service request management system exists and how it is being used. Review how management has documented how the system is to be used. Review a sample of service requests, to consider whether the requests were addressed (recorded, verified, approved and fulfilled) in a timely manner.	DSS02.01 DSS02.02 DSS02.03 DSS02.06 DSS02.07

Managed Data (APO01, APO14, DSS01, DSS04, DSS05)

Control Guidance

Control objective—Controls provide reasonable assurance that data recorded, processed and reported remain complete, accurate and valid throughout the update and storage process.

Rationale—Managing data includes the controls and procedures used to support information integrity, including its completeness, accuracy, authorization and existence. Controls are designed to support initiating, recording, processing and reporting financial information. Deficiencies in this area could significantly impact financial reporting. For instance, without appropriate authorization controls over the initiation of transactions, resulting financial information may not be reliable.

Figure A.15—Managed Data (APO01, APO14, DSS01, DSS04, DSS05)		
Control Objectives	**Control Activities to Test**	**COBIT 2019 References**
Data management strategy exists that defines how the organization manages and improves its data assets for systems significant in financial reporting. ✯	Review the organization's data management strategy. Determine whether roles and responsibilities for data management are properly defined and assigned. Determine whether the data management strategy covers the data management objectives, scope and priorities.	APO14.01
Data quality strategy exists to achieve and maintain the level of data quality (such as complexity, integrity, accuracy, completeness, validity, traceability and timeliness) required to support the business goals and objectives related to financial reporting. ✯	Determine whether the data quality strategy exists and is followed across the organization and is accompanied by corresponding policies, processes and guidelines.	APO14.04

Figure A.15—Managed Data (APO01, APO14, DSS01, DSS04, DSS05) *(cont.)*		
Control Objectives	**Control Activities to Test**	**COBIT 2019 References**
A systematic approach exists to measure and evaluate data quality according to processes and techniques, and against data quality rules related to financial reporting. ✯	Determine whether the data quality assessments are conducted according to an approved frequency per the data quality assessment policy. Obtain samples of data quality assessment reports.	APO14.06
Mechanisms, rules, processes and methods exist to validate and correct data according to predefined business rules (data cleansing). ✯	Ensure that a data cleansing policy exists. Determine whether data cleansing is conducted on a periodic basis as per the frequency defined in the data cleansing policy. Ensure that data change history is maintained through cleansing activities.	APO14.07
Ensure that the organization understands, maps, inventories and controls its data flows through business processes related to financial reporting over the data life cycle, from creation or acquisition to retirement. ✯	Verify that business process-to-data mappings are defined and maintained. Ensure the implementation of data flows and full data-to-process life cycle maps for shared data for each major business process related to financial reporting at the organizational level.	APO14.08
Policies and procedures exist for the distribution and retention of data and reporting output.	Review the policies and procedures for the distribution and retention of data and reporting output. Determine whether the policies and procedures are adequate for the protection of data and the timely distribution of the correct financial reports (including electronic reports) to appropriate personnel. Obtain and test evidence that the controls over the protection of data and the timely distribution of financial reports (including electronic reports) to appropriate personnel are operating effectively.	APO01.07 APO01.09 APO14.09 APO14.10 DSS01.01
Management protects sensitive information—logically and physically, in storage and during transmission—against unauthorized access or modification. ✯	Review the results of security testing. Determine whether there are adequate controls to protect sensitive information—logically and physically, in storage and during transmission—against unauthorized access or modification.	DSS05.06
Retention periods and storage terms are defined for documents, data, programs, reports and messages (incoming and outgoing), as well as the data (keys, certificates) used for their encryption and authentication. ✯	Obtain the procedures dealing with distribution and retention of data. Confirm that the procedures define the retention periods and storage terms for documents, data, programs, reports and messages (incoming and outgoing), as well as the data (keys, certificates) used for their encryption and authentication. Confirm that the retention periods are in conformity with the Sarbanes-Oxley Act and other regulatory requirements for data retention. Confirm that the retention periods of previously archived material are in conformity with the Sarbanes-Oxley Act. Select a sample of archived material and test evidence that archived material is being archived in conformance with the requirements of the Sarbanes-Oxley Act.	APO01.07 APO14.09 APO14.10

Figure A.15—Managed Data (APO01, APO14, DSS01, DSS04, DSS05) *(cont.)*		
Control Objectives	**Control Activities to Test**	**COBIT 2019 References**
Management has implemented a strategy for cyclical backup of data and programs. ★	Determine whether the enterprise has procedures in place to back up data and programs based on IT and user requirements. Select a sample of data files and programs and determine whether they are being backed up as required. Determine whether there are procedures to handle unsuccessful backup runs.	APO14.10 DSS04.07
The restoration of information is periodically tested. ★	Inquire whether the retention and storage of messages, documents, programs, etc., have been tested during the past year. Obtain and review the results of testing activities. Establish whether any deficiencies were noted and whether they have been reexamined. Obtain the enterprise access security policy and discuss with those responsible whether they follow such standards and guidelines dealing with sensitive backup data.	APO14.10 DSS04.07

Managed Operations (BAI04, DSS01)

Control Guidance

Control objective—Controls provide reasonable assurance that authorized programs are executed as planned and deviations from scheduled processing are identified and investigated, including controls over job scheduling, processing and error monitoring.

Rationale—Managing operations addresses how an enterprise maintains reliable application systems in support of the business to initiate, record, process and report financial information. Deficiencies in this area could significantly impact an entity's financial reporting. For instance, lapses in the continuity of application systems may prevent an enterprise from recording financial transactions and thereby undermine its integrity.

Figure A.16—Managed Operations (BAI04, DSS01)		
Control Objectives	**Control Activities to Test**	**COBIT 2019 References**
Management has established, documented and maintained operational procedures reliably and consistently. ★	Determine whether management has documented its procedures for IT operations, and operations are reviewed periodically for compliance. Review a sample of events to confirm that response procedures are operating effectively. When used, review the job scheduling process and the procedures in place to monitor job completeness.	DSS01.01
System event data are sufficiently retained to provide chronological information and logs to enable the review, examination and reconstruction of system and data processing.	Determine whether sufficient chronological information is being recorded and stored in logs, and is usable for reconstruction, if necessary. Obtain a sample of the log entries, to determine whether they sufficiently allow for reconstruction. Determine whether system capacity and availability are monitored and documented.	BAI04.04 DSS01.03

Figure A.16—Managed Operations (BAI04, DSS01) *(cont.)*

Control Objectives	Control Activities to Test	COBIT 2019 References
System event data are designed to provide reasonable assurance as to the completeness and timeliness of system and data processing.	Inquire as to the type of information that is used by management to determine the completeness and timeliness of system and data processing. Review a sample of system processing event data to confirm the completeness and timeliness of processing. Confirm whether system capacity and availability issues are investigated and addressed.	BAI04.05 DSS01.01 DSS01.03

End-User Computing (APO14, DSS04, DSS05, DSS06)

Control Guidance

The following illustrative controls for end-user computing have been extracted from the control guidance in **figures A.5** to **A.16** and are presented to address the characteristics of a typical end-user computing environment. Appropriate COBIT processes apply to this environment.

Figure A.17—End-user Computing (APO14, DSS04, DSS05, DSS06)

Control Objectives	Control Activities to Test	COBIT 2019 References
End-user computing policies and procedures concerning security and processing integrity exist and are followed. ☆	Obtain a copy of the end-user computing policies and procedures and confirm that they address security and processing integrity controls. Select a sample of users and inquire whether they are aware of this policy and whether they are in compliance with it.	DSS05.03
End-user computing, including spreadsheets and other user-developed programs, are documented and regularly reviewed for processing integrity, including their ability to sort, summarize and report accurately. ☆	Inquire as to management's knowledge of end-user programs in use across the company. Inquire as to the frequency and approaches followed to review end-user programs for processing integrity, and review a sample of these to confirm effectiveness. Review user-developed systems and test their ability to sort, summarize and report in accordance with management intentions.	DSS05.03 DSS06.02
User-developed systems and data are regularly backed up and stored in a secure area. ☆	Inquire how end-user systems are backed up and where they are stored.	APO14.10 DSS04.07
User-developed systems, such as spreadsheets and other end-user programs, are secured from unauthorized use. ☆	Review the security used to protect unauthorized access to user-developed systems. Consider observing a user attempting to gain unauthorized access to user-developed systems. Inquire how management is able to detect unauthorized access and what follow-up procedures are performed to assess the impact of such access. Inquire whether information in storage is encrypted according to its classification.	DSS05.03 DSS06.03

Figure A.17—End-user Computing (APO14, DSS04, DSS05, DSS06) *(cont.)*		
Control Objectives	**Control Activities to Test**	**COBIT 2019 References**
Inputs, processing and outputs from user-developed systems are independently verified for completeness and accuracy. ✯	Inquire how management verifies the accuracy and completeness of information processed and reported from user-developed systems. Inquire as to who reviews and approves outputs from user-developed systems prior to their submission for further processing or final reporting. Consider reperforming or reviewing the logic used in user-developed systems and conclude on their ability to process completely and accurately.	DSS06.02

APPENDIX B
COBIT 2019 Governance and Management Objectives Mapped to COSO Components and Principles

The purpose of this appendix is to expand on the COBIT 2019 high-level mappings to the COSO framework that are shown in **figure 3.4** in Chapter 3. The mapping in **figure B.1** is at the control objective level (governance and management practice) and includes only the SOX selection.

Figure B.1—Summary COBIT Areas/COSO Components

				COSO Component																
				Control Environment					Risk Assessment				Control Activities			Information and Communication			Monitoring Activities	
				Principles																
Entity Level	Activity Level	Detailed Activity/Objective Level	COBIT 2019 Reference	1	2	3	4	5	6	7	8	9	10	11	12	13	14	15	16	17
		Evaluate, Direct and Monitor (EDM) (IT Environment)																		
		Ensured Governance Framework Setting and Maintenance	EDM01																	
•		Evaluate the governance system.	EDM01.01	•	•	•		•	•	•	•					•	•			
•		Direct the governance system.	EDM01.02	•	•	•		•								•	•			
•		Monitor the governance system.	EDM01.03													•	•		•	•
		Ensured Risk Optimization	EDM03																	
•		Evaluate risk management.	EDM03.01		•		•	•	•	•						•	•			
•		Direct risk management.	EDM03.02		•			•	•	•						•	•			
•		Monitor risk management.	EDM03.03		•			•	•	•						•	•		•	•
		Ensured Stakeholder Engagement	EDM05																	
•		Direct stakeholder engagement, communication and reporting.	EDM05.02		•			•								•	•			
•		Monitor stakeholder engagement.	EDM05.03													•	•	•	•	•
		Align, Plan and Organize (APO) (IT Environment)																		
		Managed I&T Management Framework	APO01																	
•		Design the management system for enterprise I&T.	APO01.01	•		•			•	•	•									
•		Communicate management objectives, direction and decisions made.	APO01.02	•		•	•									•	•			
•		Establish roles and responsibilities.	APO01.05			•	•	•								•	•			
•	•	Define information (data) and system ownership.	APO01.07								•					•	•			
		Define and communicate policies and procedures.	APO01.09														•			
		Managed Strategy	APO02																	
		Understand enterprise context and direction.	APO02.01						•							•	•			

Figure B.1—Summary COBIT Areas/COSO Components *(cont.)*

Entity Level	Activity Level	Detailed Activity/Objective Level	COBIT 2019 Reference	COSO Component																
				Control Environment					Risk Assessment				Control Activities			Information and Communication			Monitoring Activities	
				Principles																
				1	2	3	4	5	6	7	8	9	10	11	12	13	14	15	16	17
•		Assess current capabilities, performance and digital maturity of the enterprise.	APO02.02						•							•	•			
•		Define target digital capabilities.	APO02.03						•							•	•			
•		Conduct a gap analysis.	APO02.04						•							•	•			
•		Define the strategic plan and road map.	APO02.05				•	•	•							•	•		•	
•		Communicate the I&T strategy and direction.	APO02.06					•								•	•			
		Managed Human Resources	APO07																	
•		Acquire and maintain adequate and appropriate staffing.	APO07.01				•				•				•					
•		Identify key IT personnel.	APO07.02								•		•		•					
•		Maintain the skills and competencies of personnel.	APO07.03	•			•												•	
•		Plan and track the usage of IT and business human resources.	APO07.05				•				•					•	•			
		Managed Service Agreements	APO09																	
	•	Identify I&T services.	APO09.01						•				•	•		•	•			
	•	Catalog I&T-enabled services.	APO09.02						•				•	•		•	•			
	•	Define and prepare service agreements.	APO09.03						•				•	•		•	•			
	•	Monitor and report service levels.	APO09.04					•	•				•	•		•	•		•	•
	•	Review service agreements and contracts.	APO09.05										•	•		•	•	•		
		Managed Vendors	APO10																	
	•	Identify and evaluate vendor relationships and contracts.	APO10.01						•				•	•		•	•			
	•	Select vendors.	APO10.02						•				•	•		•	•			
	•	Manage vendor relationships and contracts.	APO10.03					•	•				•	•		•	•			
	•	Manage vendor risk.	APO10.04					•	•	•	•	•	•	•		•	•			
•	•	Monitor vendor performance and compliance.	APO10.05										•	•		•	•	•	•	•
		Managed Quality	APO11																	
•		Establish a quality management system (QMS).	APO11.01					•	•										•	•
•		Focus quality management on customers.	APO11.02					•	•						•	•				

Figure B.1—Summary COBIT Areas/COSO Components *(cont.)*

Entity Level	Activity Level	Detailed Activity/Objective Level	COBIT 2019 Reference	COSO Component																
				Control Environment					Risk Assessment				Control Activities			Information and Communication			Monitoring Activities	
				Principles																
				1	2	3	4	5	6	7	8	9	10	11	12	13	14	15	16	17
•		Manage quality standards, practices and procedures and integrate quality management into key processes and solutions.	APO11.03					•	•						•	•				
•		Perform quality monitoring, control and reviews.	APO11.04					•	•								•		•	•
•		Maintain continuous improvement.	APO11.05					•	•							•				
		Managed Risk	APO12																	
•		Collect data.	APO12.01						•	•	•	•				•	•			
•		Analyze risk.	APO12.02						•	•	•	•				•	•			
•		Maintain a risk profile.	APO12.03						•	•	•	•				•	•			
•		Articulate risk.	APO12.04						•	•	•	•				•	•			
•		Define a risk management action portfolio.	APO12.05					•	•	•	•	•				•	•			
•		Respond to risk.	APO12.06						•	•	•	•				•	•			
		Managed Security	APO13																	
	•	Establish and maintain an information security management system (ISMS).	APO13.01					•	•	•	•	•		•		•	•			
•	•	Define and manage an information security and privacy risk treatment plan.	APO13.02						•	•	•	•		•		•	•			
•	•	Monitor and review the information security management system (ISMS).	APO13.03						•	•	•	•		•		•	•			
		Managed Data	APO14																	
•	•	Define and communicate the organization's data management strategy and roles and responsibilities.	APO14.01		•	•		•	•	•	•	•				•	•			
	•	Define a data quality strategy.	APO14.04						•	•	•	•				•	•			
	•	Ensure a data quality assessment approach.	APO14.06						•	•	•	•		•		•	•		•	•
	•	Define the data cleansing approach.	APO14.07					•	•	•	•	•		•	•	•	•			
	•	Manage the life cycle of data assets.	APO14.08						•	•	•	•		•		•	•			
	•	Support data archiving and retention.	APO14.09						•	•	•	•		•		•	•			
	•	Manage data backup and restore arrangements.	APO14.10						•	•	•	•		•		•	•			

Figure B.1—Summary COBIT Areas/COSO Components *(cont.)*

Entity Level	Activity Level	Detailed Activity/Objective Level	COBIT 2019 Reference	COSO Component																
				Control Environment					Risk Assessment				Control Activities			Information and Communication			Monitoring Activities	
				Principles																
				1	2	3	4	5	6	7	8	9	10	11	12	13	14	15	16	17
		Build, Acquire and Implement (BAI) (Program Development and Program Change)																		
		Managed Requirements Definition	BAI02																	
	•	Define and maintain business functional and technical requirements.	BAI02.01						•			•	•	•		•	•			
	•	Perform a feasibility study and formulate alternative solutions.	BAI02.02						•			•	•	•		•	•			
	•	Manage requirements risk.	BAI02.03						•			•	•	•		•	•			
	•	Obtain approval of requirements and solutions.	BAI02.04						•			•	•	•		•	•			
		Managed Solutions Identification and Build	BAI03																	
	•	Design high-level solutions.	BAI03.01						•				•	•		•	•			
	•	Design detailed solution components.	BAI03.02						•				•	•		•	•			
	•	Develop solution components.	BAI03.03						•			•	•	•		•	•			
	•	Procure solution components.	BAI03.04						•			•	•	•		•	•			
	•	Build solutions.	BAI03.05						•			•	•	•		•	•			
•	•	Perform quality assurance (QA).	BAI03.06						•			•	•	•		•	•		•	•
	•	Prepare for solution testing.	BAI03.07						•			•	•	•		•	•			
	•	Execute solution testing.	BAI03.08						•			•	•	•		•	•			
	•	Manage changes to requirements.	BAI03.09						•			•	•	•		•	•			
	•	Maintain solutions.	BAI03.10						•				•	•		•	•			
	•	Define IT products and services and maintain the service portfolio.	BAI03.11										•	•		•	•			
	•	Design solutions based on the defined development methodology.	BAI03.12										•	•		•	•			
		Managed Availability and Capacity	BAI04																	
	•	Assess current availability, performance and capacity to create a baseline.	BAI04.01									•	•	•		•	•			
	•	Assess business impact.	BAI04.02									•	•	•		•	•			
	•	Plan for new or changed service requirements.	BAI04.03									•	•	•		•	•			
	•	Monitor and review availability and capacity.	BAI04.04									•	•	•		•	•		•	•
	•	Investigate and address availability, performance and capacity issues.	BAI04.05									•	•	•		•	•			
		Managed IT Changes	BAI06																	
	•	Evaluate, prioritize and authorize change requests.	BAI06.01						•		•	•	•	•		•	•			

Figure B.1—Summary COBIT Areas/COSO Components *(cont.)*

Entity Level	Activity Level	Detailed Activity/Objective Level	COBIT 2019 Reference	COSO Component: Control Environment					Risk Assessment				Control Activities			Information and Communication			Monitoring Activities	
				Principles: 1	2	3	4	5	6	7	8	9	10	11	12	13	14	15	16	17
	•	Manage emergency changes.	BAI06.02						•		•	•	•	•		•	•			
	•	Track and report change status.	BAI06.03						•		•	•	•	•		•	•			
	•	Close and document the changes.	BAI06.04						•		•	•	•	•		•	•			
		Managed IT Change Acceptance and Transitioning	BAI07																	
	•	Establish an implementation plan.	BAI07.01						•			•	•	•		•	•			
	•	Plan business process, system and data conversion.	BAI07.02						•			•	•	•		•	•			
	•	Plan acceptance tests.	BAI07.03						•			•	•	•		•	•			
	•	Establish a test environment.	BAI07.04						•			•	•	•		•	•			
	•	Perform acceptance tests.	BAI07.05						•			•	•	•		•	•			
	•	Promote to production and manage releases.	BAI07.06						•	•	•	•	•	•		•	•			
	•	Provide early production support.	BAI07.07						•			•	•	•		•	•			
	•	Perform a postimplementation review.	BAI07.08									•	•	•		•	•			
		Managed Configuration	BAI10																	
	•	Establish and maintain a configuration model.	BAI10.01						•		•	•	•	•		•	•			
	•	Establish and maintain a configuration repository and baseline.	BAI10.02						•		•	•	•	•		•	•			
	•	Maintain and control configuration items.	BAI10.03						•		•	•	•	•		•	•			
	•	Produce status and configuration reports.	BAI10.04						•		•	•	•	•		•	•			
		Managed Projects	BAI11																	
•	•	Manage project quality.	BAI11.05													•			•	•
		Deliver, Service and Support (DSS) (Operations and Access to Programs and Data)																		
		Managed Operations (including outsourced services)	DSS01																	
	•	Perform operational procedures.	DSS01.01						•				•	•	•	•	•			
•	•	Manage outsourced I&T services.	DSS01.02						•	•	•	•	•	•		•	•			
	•	Monitor I&T infrastructure.	DSS01.03						•				•	•		•	•			
		Managed Service Requests and Incidents	DSS02																	
	•	Define classification schemes for incidents and service requests.	DSS02.01						•				•	•		•	•			
	•	Record, classify and prioritize requests and incidents.	DSS02.02						•				•	•		•	•			
	•	Verify, approve and fulfill service requests.	DSS02.03						•				•	•		•	•			

Figure B.1—Summary COBIT Areas/COSO Components *(cont.)*

Entity Level	Activity Level	Detailed Activity/Objective Level	COBIT 2019 Reference	COSO Component																
				Control Environment					Risk Assessment				Control Activities			Information and Communication			Monitoring Activities	
				Principles																
				1	2	3	4	5	6	7	8	9	10	11	12	13	14	15	16	17
	•	Investigate, diagnose and allocate incidents.	DSS02.04						•				•	•		•	•			
	•	Resolve and recover from incidents.	DSS02.05						•				•	•		•	•			
	•	Close service requests and incidents.	DSS02.06						•				•	•		•	•			
	•	Track status and produce reports.	DSS02.07						•				•	•		•	•		•	•
		Managed Problems	DSS03																	
	•	Identify and classify problems.	DSS03.01						•				•	•		•	•			
	•	Investigate and diagnose problems.	DSS03.02						•				•	•		•	•			
	•	Raise known errors.	DSS03.03						•				•	•		•	•			
	•	Resolve and close problems.	DSS03.04						•				•	•		•	•			
	•	Perform proactive problem management.	DSS03.05						•				•	•		•	•			
		Managed Continuity	DSS04																	
	•	Manage backup arrangements.	DSS04.07						•				•	•		•	•			
		Managed Security Services	DSS05																	
	•	Protect against malicious software.	DSS05.01					•	•	•	•		•	•		•	•			
	•	Manage network and connectivity security.	DSS05.02					•	•	•	•		•	•		•	•			
	•	Manage endpoint security.	DSS05.03					•	•	•	•		•	•		•	•			
	•	Manage user identity and logical access.	DSS05.04						•	•	•		•	•		•	•			
	•	Manage sensitive documents and output devices.	DSS05.06					•	•	•	•		•	•		•	•			
	•	Manage vulnerabilities and monitor the infrastructure for security-related events.	DSS05.07						•	•	•		•	•		•	•		•	•
		Managed Business Process Controls (including application controls)	DSS06																	
	•	Align control activities embedded in business processes with enterprise objectives.	DSS06.01						•				•	•		•	•			
	•	Control the processing of information.	DSS06.02						•				•	•		•	•			
	•	Manage roles, responsibilities, access privileges and levels of authority.	DSS06.03					•	•	•	•		•	•		•	•			
	•	Manage errors and exceptions.	DSS06.04						•				•	•		•	•			
	•	Ensure traceability and accountability for information events.	DSS06.05						•				•	•		•	•			

Figure B.1—Summary COBIT Areas/COSO Components *(cont.)*

Entity Level	Activity Level	Detailed Activity/Objective Level	COBIT 2019 Reference	COSO Component																
				Control Environment					Risk Assessment				Control Activities			Information and Communication			Monitoring Activities	
				Principles																
				1	2	3	4	5	6	7	8	9	10	11	12	13	14	15	16	17
Monitor, Evaluate and Assess (MEA) (IT Environment)																				
		Managed Performance and Conformance Monitoring	MEA01																	
•		Establish a monitoring approach.	MEA01.01						•							•	•		•	•
•		Set performance and conformance targets.	MEA01.02						•							•	•		•	•
•		Collect and process performance and conformance data.	MEA01.03						•							•	•		•	•
•		Analyze and report performance.	MEA01.04						•							•	•		•	•
•		Ensure the implementation of corrective actions.	MEA01.05					•	•							•	•		•	•
		Managed System of Internal Control	MEA02																	
•	•	Monitor internal controls.	MEA02.01													•	•		•	•
•		Review effectiveness of business process controls.	MEA02.02					•	•	•	•	•	•			•	•		•	•
•		Identify and report control deficiencies.	MEA02.04					•	•							•	•		•	•
		Managed Compliance With External Requirements	MEA03																	
•		Identify external compliance requirements.	MEA03.01								•					•	•		•	•
•		Obtain assurance of external compliance.	MEA03.02					•			•				•	•	•		•	•
		Managed Assurance	MEA04																	
•		Ensure that assurance providers are independent and qualified.	MEA04.01	•	•	•	•	•								•	•		•	•
•		Develop risk-based planning of assurance initiatives.	MEA04.02						•	•	•	•				•	•		•	•
•		Define the scope of the assurance initiative.	MEA04.04													•	•		•	•
•		Define the work program for the assurance initiative.	MEA04.05						•	•	•	•	•			•	•		•	•
•		Execute the assurance initiative, focusing on design effectiveness.	MEA04.06				•	•	•	•	•	•				•	•			
•		Execute the assurance initiative, focusing on operating effectiveness.	MEA04.07						•	•	•	•				•	•			
•		Report and follow up on the assurance initiative.	MEA04.08										•			•	•		•	•
•		Follow up on recommendations and actions.	MEA04.09										•			•	•		•	•

Source: Adapted from ISACA, *IT Control Objectives for Sarbanes-Oxley: Using COBIT® 5 in the Design and Implementation of Internal Controls Over Financial Reporting*, 3rd Edition, USA, 2014, *https://store.isaca.org/s/store#/store/browse/detail/a2S4w000004Ko9JEAS*

Page intentionally left blank

APPENDIX C
Example Application Controls

Chapter 4 introduces and defines application controls. To assist enterprises in applying an automated control approach, examples of automated controls are provided in **figures C.2** through **C.9** in this appendix. For the most part, these controls can be enabled through the use of built-in application control functionality. This functionality is commonly found in integrated ERP environments, such as SAP®, Oracle® NetSuite®, MS Dynamics®, Aptean® Axis® ERP and others.

Where this functionality does not exist, these control objectives may require a combination of manual and automated control procedures to satisfy the control objective.

The control objectives presented in **figures C.2** through **C.9** should not be considered an exhaustive list, but rather examples of controls that are commonly enabled by application systems. Enterprises should consider what additional control objectives are required, based on their particular industry and operating environment.

Figures C.2 through **C.9** refer to controls that extend into applications and business processes that contribute to financial statement assertions, including completeness, accuracy, valuation and authorization controls. Definitions and some examples of these financial statement assertions are summarized in **figure C.1**.

Figure C.1—Financial Statement Assertion Definitions and Examples

Financial Statement Assertions	Definition	Example
Existence	Assertions about existence or occurrence address whether assets or liabilities of the entity exist at a given date and whether recorded transactions have occurred during a given period.	Management asserts that finished goods inventories in the balance sheet are available for sale. Similarly, management asserts that sales in the income statement represent the exchange of goods or services with customers for cash or other consideration.
Completeness	Assertions about completeness address whether all transactions and accounts that should be presented in the financial statements are included.	Management asserts that all purchases of goods and services are recorded and are included in the financial statements. Similarly, management asserts that notes payable in the balance sheet include all such obligations of the entity.
Valuation	Assertions about valuation or allocation address whether asset, liability, equity, revenue and expense components have been included in the financial statements in appropriate amounts.	Management asserts that property is recorded at historical cost and that such cost is systematically allocated to appropriate accounting periods. Similarly, management asserts that trade accounts receivable included in the balance sheet are stated at net realizable value. Statements are properly classified and described.

Figure C.2—Application Control Objectives for the Financial Statement

Illustrative Control Objectives	Financial Assertions
Entries booked in the close process are complete and accurate.	Completeness Existence
Automated amortization timing, periods and methods are appropriate and accurately entered.	Valuation Existence

Figure C.2—Application Control Objectives for the Financial Statement *(cont.)*

Illustrative Control Objectives	Financial Assertions
Variance reports are generated to identify posting errors/out-of-balance conditions.	Completeness Existence Valuation
Standard, recurring period-end journal entries submitted from subsidiary ledger systems are automated, appropriately approved and entered accurately.	Completeness Existence Valuation
Systems generate reports of all recurring and nonrecurring journal entries.	Completeness Existence
All nonstandard journal entries are tracked and are appropriate.	Completeness Existence
Account codes and transaction amounts are accurate and complete, with exceptions reported.	Completeness Existence
General ledger balances reconcile to subledger balances.	Completeness Existence
Recorded amounts undergo an automated comparison to predicted amounts.	Completeness Existence
Out-of-balance entries are prohibited.	Completeness Existence
Enterprisewide consolidation, including standard intercompany eliminations, is automated/performed using a third-party software product.	Completeness Existence Valuation
System functionality supports the segregation of the posting and approval functions.	Existence
Access to general ledger records is appropriate and authorized.	Completeness Existence Valuation
Transactions cannot be recorded outside of financial close cutoff requirements.	Completeness Existence Valuation
Annually approved recurring accruals are accurately booked in the appropriate periods.	Completeness Existence Valuation
System controls are in place for appropriate approval of write-offs.	Existence
Interrelated balance sheets and income statement accounts undergo automated reconciliation.	Completeness Existence
The sources of all entries are readily identifiable.	Existence
Transactions are either rejected, or accepted and identified, on exception reports in the event of data exceptions.	Completeness Existence
Account mappings are up to date.	Existence

Figure C.3—Application Control Objectives for the General Ledger

Illustrative Control Objectives	Financial Assertions
Access to general ledger entries is appropriate and authorized.	Completeness Existence Valuation

Figure C.3—Application Control Objectives for the General Ledger *(cont.)*	
Illustrative Control Objectives	**Financial Assertions**
General ledger balances reconcile to subledger balances and such reconciliations are reviewed for accuracy and approved by supervisory personnel.	Completeness Existence
Interrelated balance sheets and income statement accounts undergo automated reconciliations to confirm accuracy of such accounts.	Completeness Existence
Systems generate reports of all recurring and nonrecurring journal entries for review by management for accuracy.	Completeness Existence
System functionality exists to segregate the posting and approval functions.	Existence
All nonstandard journal entries are tracked and are appropriate.	Completeness Existence
Account codes and transaction amounts are accurate and complete, with exceptions reported.	Completeness Existence
Recorded amounts undergo automated comparison to predicted amounts to confirm accuracy of entries.	Completeness Existence
Out-of-balance entries are prohibited.	Completeness Existence
Enterprisewide consolidation, including standard intercompany eliminations, is automated/performed.	Completeness Existence Valuation
Variance reports are generated to identify posting errors/out-of-balance conditions.	Completeness Existence Valuation
System controls are in place for appropriate approval of write-offs.	Existence
Journal entries of exceptional amounts that were posted to the general ledger during the month are flagged by the system and subsequently reviewed for accuracy and approved by the controller or CFO after month-end.	Completeness Existence Valuation
A report of all journal entries completed as part of the closing process is reviewed by management to confirm the completeness and appropriateness of all recorded entries.	Completeness Existence
General ledger master file change reports are generated by the system and reviewed as necessary by an individual who does not input the changes.	Completeness Existence
Actual-to-actual, actual-to-budget and yield reports are produced from the general ledger system on a monthly basis prior to the final close of the general ledger. Reports are distributed to and reviewed by the controller and CFO. Unusual amounts or variances are investigated and reclassified when applicable.	Completeness Existence Valuation
A standard chart of accounts has been approved by management and is utilized within all entities of the corporation. Adding to or deleting from the general ledger is limited to authorized accounting department personnel.	Completeness Existence
A stale items report (e.g., reconciling items outstanding over 90 days) is generated by the system to monitor timely follow-up and resolution of outstanding items.	Completeness Existence
Entries booked in the close process are complete and accurate.	Completeness Existence
Automated amortization timing, periods and methods are appropriate and accurately entered.	Valuation Existence
Standard, recurring period-end journal entries submitted from subsidiary ledger systems are automated, appropriately approved and entered accurately.	Completeness Existence Valuation

Figure C.3—Application Control Objectives for the General Ledger *(cont.)*

Illustrative Control Objectives	Financial Assertions
Transactions cannot be recorded outside of financial close cutoff requirements.	Completeness Existence Valuation
Annually approved recurring accruals are accurately booked in the appropriate periods.	Completeness Existence Valuation
The sources of all entries are readily identifiable.	Existence
Transactions are rejected, or accepted and identified, on exception reports in the event of data exceptions.	Completeness Existence
Account mappings are up to date.	Existence

Figure C.4—Application Control Objectives for Order to Cash

Illustrative Control Objectives	Financial Assertions
Orders are processed only within approved customer credit limits.	Valuation
Orders are approved by management as to prices and terms of sale.	Existence
Orders and cancellations of orders are input accurately.	Valuation
Order entry data are transferred completely and accurately to the shipping and invoicing activities.	Valuation Completeness
All orders received from customers are input and processed.	Completeness
Only valid orders are input and processed.	Existence
Invoices are generated using authorized terms and prices.	Valuation
Invoices are accurately calculated and recorded.	Valuation
Credit notes and adjustments to accounts receivable are accurately calculated and recorded.	Valuation
All goods shipped are invoiced.	Completeness
Credit notes for all goods returned and adjustments to accounts receivable are issued in accordance with enterprise policy.	Existence
Invoices relate to valid shipments.	Existence
All credit notes relate to a return of goods or other valid adjustments.	Completeness
All invoices issued are recorded.	Completeness
All credit notes issued are recorded.	Existence
Invoices are recorded in the appropriate period.	Valuation
Credit notes issued are recorded in the appropriate period.	Valuation
Cash receipts are recorded in the period in which they are received.	Valuation
Cash receipts data are entered for processing accurately.	Valuation
All cash receipts data are entered for processing.	Existence
Cash receipts data are valid and are entered for processing only once.	Completeness
Cash discounts are accurately calculated and recorded.	Valuation
Timely collection of accounts receivable is monitored.	Valuation
The customer master file is maintained.	Completeness Existence

Figure C.5—Application Control Objectives for Purchase to Pay	
Illustrative Control Objectives	**Financial Assertions**
Purchase orders are placed only for approved acquisitions.	Existence
Purchase orders are accurately entered.	Valuation
All purchase orders issued are input and processed.	Completeness
Amounts posted to accounts payable represent goods or services received.	Existence
Accounts payable amounts are accurately calculated and recorded.	Valuation
All amounts for goods or services received are input and processed to accounts payable.	Completeness
Amounts for goods or services received are recorded in the appropriate period.	Valuation
Accounts payable are adjusted only for valid reasons.	Completeness Existence
Credit notes and other adjustments are accurately calculated and recorded.	Valuation
All valid credit notes and other adjustments related to accounts payable are input and processed.	Completeness Existence
Credit notes and other adjustments are recorded in the appropriate period.	Valuation
Disbursements are made only for goods and services received.	Existence
Disbursements are distributed to the appropriate suppliers.	Existence
Disbursements are accurately calculated and recorded.	Valuation
All disbursements are recorded.	Completeness
Disbursements are recorded in the period in which they are issued.	Valuation
Only valid changes are made to the supplier master file.	Completeness Existence
All valid changes to the supplier master file are input and processed.	Completeness Existence
Changes to the supplier master file are accurate.	Valuation
Changes to the supplier master file are processed in a timely manner.	Completeness Existence
Supplier master file data remain up to date.	Completeness Existence

Figure C.6—Application Control Objectives for the Inventory Cycle	
Illustrative Control Objectives	**Financial Assertions**
Adjustments to inventory prices or quantities are recorded promptly and in the appropriate period.	Existence Completeness Valuation
Adjustments to inventory prices or quantities are recorded accurately.	Valuation
Raw materials are received and accepted only if they have valid purchase orders.	Existence
Raw materials received are recorded accurately.	Valuation
All raw materials received are recorded.	Completeness
Receipts of raw materials are recorded promptly and in the appropriate period.	Valuation
Defective raw materials are returned promptly to suppliers.	Existence
All transfers of raw materials to production are recorded accurately and in the appropriate period.	Valuation Completeness

Figure C.6—Application Control Objectives for the Inventory Cycle *(cont.)*	
Illustrative Control Objectives	**Financial Assertions**
All direct and indirect expenses associated with production are recorded accurately and in the appropriate period.	Valuation
All transfers of completed units of production to finished goods inventory are recorded completely and accurately in the appropriate period.	Valuation Completeness
Finished goods returned by customers are recorded completely and accurately in the appropriate period.	Valuation Completeness
Finished goods received from production are recorded completely and accurately in the appropriate period.	Completeness Valuation
All shipments are recorded.	Existence
Shipments are recorded accurately.	Valuation
Shipments are recorded promptly and in the appropriate period.	Valuation
Inventory is reduced only when goods are shipped with approved customer orders.	Completeness Existence
Costs of shipped inventory are transferred from inventory to cost of sales.	Existence Valuation
Costs of shipped inventory are accurately recorded.	Valuation
Amounts posted to cost of sales represent those associated with shipped inventory.	Completeness Existence
Costs of shipped inventory are transferred from inventory to cost of sales promptly and in the appropriate period.	Valuation
Only valid changes are made to the inventory management master file.	Existence Completeness
All valid changes to the inventory management master file are input and processed.	Existence Completeness
Changes to the inventory management master file are accurate.	Valuation
Changes to the inventory management master file are promptly processed.	Existence Completeness
Inventory management master file data remain up to date.	Completeness Existence

Figure C.7—Application Control Objectives for the Fixed Asset Cycle	
Illustrative Control Objectives	**Financial Assertions**
Fixed asset acquisitions are accurately recorded.	Valuation
Fixed asset acquisitions are recorded in the appropriate period.	Valuation
All fixed asset acquisitions are recorded.	Completeness
Depreciation charges are accurately calculated and recorded.	Valuation
All depreciation charges are recorded in the appropriate period.	Existence Valuation Completeness
All fixed asset disposals are recorded.	Existence
Fixed asset disposals are accurately calculated and recorded.	Valuation
Fixed asset disposals are recorded in the appropriate period.	Valuation
Records of fixed asset maintenance activity are accurately maintained.	Completeness
Fixed asset maintenance activity records are updated in a timely manner.	Completeness

Figure C.7—Application Control Objectives for the Fixed Asset Cycle *(cont.)*	
Illustrative Control Objectives	**Financial Assertions**
Only valid changes are made to the fixed asset register and/or master file.	Completeness Existence
All valid changes to the fixed asset register and/or master file are input and processed.	Completeness Existence
Changes to the fixed asset register and/or master file are accurate.	Valuation
Changes to the fixed asset register and/or master file are promptly processed.	Completeness Existence
Fixed asset register and/or master file data remain up to date.	Completeness Existence

Figure C.8—Application Control Objectives for Human Resources	
Illustrative Control Objectives	**Financial Assertions**
Additions to the payroll master files represent valid employees.	Existence
All new employees are added to the payroll master files. Terminated employees are removed from the payroll master files.	Completeness Existence
Employees are terminated only within statutory and union requirements.	Completeness
Deletions from the payroll master files represent valid terminations.	Completeness
All time worked is input.	Completeness
Time worked is accurately input and processed.	Valuation
Payroll is recorded in the appropriate period.	Valuation
Payroll (including compensation and withholding) is accurately calculated and recorded.	Valuation
Payroll is disbursed to appropriate employees.	Existence
Only valid changes are made to the payroll master files.	Existence Completeness
All valid changes to the payroll master files are input and processed.	Existence Completeness
Changes to the payroll master files are accurate.	Valuation
Changes to the payroll master files are processed in a timely manner.	Existence Completeness
Payroll master file data remain up to date.	Existence Completeness
Only valid changes are made to the payroll withholding tables.	Existence Completeness
All valid changes to the payroll withholding tables are input and processed.	Existence Completeness
Changes to the payroll withholding tables are accurate.	Valuation
Changes to the payroll withholding tables are promptly processed.	Existence Completeness
Payroll withholding table data remain up to date.	Existence Completeness

Figure C.9—Application Control Objectives for Tax Accounting

Illustrative Control Objectives	Financial Assertions
Automated workflows are used for timely filing of returns.	Completeness
Tax payments are correctly calculated and recorded to the general ledger.	Completeness Valuation Existence
Tax exposures and valuation allowances are correctly calculated and recorded.	Completeness Existence Valuation
Tax expenses are recorded in the correct periods.	Completeness Existence Valuation
Permanent and temporary differences are identified and recorded accurately.	Completeness Existence Valuation
Correct book income is used in the tax accrual.	Completeness Existence
Tax assets, liabilities and expenses are complete and correctly calculated and reported.	Completeness Existence
Depreciation is calculated using appropriate bases, resulting in correct charges and tax ramifications.	Completeness Existence
Sales and use tax is calculated appropriately, correctly and in a timely manner.	Completeness Existence
Value-added tax is correctly accounted for and filed appropriately.	Completeness Existence
Transfer pricing policies are up to date and accurately represented in the systems.	Completeness Existence
All tax payments are accurately reflected in the general ledger.	Valuation
Property tax filings are timely and accurate.	Completeness Existence Valuation

APPENDIX D

Example Application and Technology Inventory

A critical step in an effective IT control compliance program, as discussed in Chapter 6, is an inventory of in-scope applications and technology infrastructure. This inventory should not be developed only once but should be maintained on an ongoing basis. **Figure D.1** reflects an example inventory. The IT compliance manager then works with the finance and business controls team to make decisions on which applications and subsystems are in scope for internal and external audits.

Figure D.1—Sample Application and Technology Layers Inventory

Application Name	Related Business Process	Application Details					Database		Operating System/Network		Hardware Platform		Physical Location		Risk Rating
		Package/ In-house	Customized	Outsourced	SSAE 16/ SOC 1 Report Availabe	Owner	Version	Owner	Version	Owner	Version	Owner	Facility	Owner	
SAP® ERP (V.6.0)	Financials	ERP Package	Yes	No	N/A	Kerry M.	Oracle® 12.2c Release 2	John G.	Solaris™ 11.3	Ryan S.	HPE ProLiant® DL580 Gen 10	Frank B.	Calgary	D'Arcy M.	
Oracle Fusion Applications Technology 11g	HR payroll	ERP Package	Yes	No	N/A	Tom M.	Oracle 12c Release 2	John G.	Solaris 11.3	Adel M.	HPE ProLiant DL580 Gen 10	Frank B.	Houston	Rhonda M.	
Sage® 300 ERP 2021	Subsidiary accounting	Package	No	No	N/A	Esther C.	Oracle 12c Release 2	John G.	HP-UX® v11 i	Adel M.	HP® 9000	Frank B.	Denver	Robert P.	
Tally Pro®	Time recording	Outsourced Processing	No	Yes	Yes	Darryl J.	Refer to SSAE 18, SOC® 1	Alan S.	Refer to SSAE 18, SOC 1	Reid C.	Refer to SSAE 18 SOC 1	Rob K.	Refer to SSAE 18, SOC 1	D'Arcy M.	
ZOHO® Invoice with Bolt on CRM Cloud	Billing	Package	No	Yes	Yes	Paul Z.	Refer to SSAE 18, SOC 1	Alan S.	IBM i™	Ryan R.	Refer to SSAE 18, SOC 1	Barb V.	Refer to SSAE 18, SOC 1	D'Arcy M.	
Sungard® Front Arena for Back Office™	Funds Administration	Outsourced processing	No	Yes	Yes	Kerry M.	Refer to SSAE 18, SOC 1	Craig T.	Refer to SSAE 18, SOC 1	Ryan S.	Refer to SSAE 18, SOC 1	Doug W.	Refer to SSAE 18, SOC 1	Doug W.	

Source: Adapted from ISACA, *IT Control Objectives for Sarbanes-Oxley: Using COBIT® 5 in the Design and Implementation of Internal Controls Over Financial Reporting, 3rd Edition*, USA, 2014, *https://store.isaca.org/s/store#/store/browse/detail/a2S4w000004Ko9JEAS*

Page intentionally left blank

APPENDIX E
Example SOX ITGC Control Matrix

SOX ITGC Control MATRIX—IT General Controls

The purpose of this example template is to act as a master SOX ITGC control matrix, which has two functions:

- For scoping purposes, to show all priority control processes that have been selected based on a risk assessment
- To summarize the findings from the control design and testing documentation

Control Area Coding

Following are the SOX ITGC control areas, their codes and their scope descriptions:

- **System development** (SD)—Includes requirements definition and solutions build
- **Manage changes** (MC)—Includes new system acceptance and transitioning
- **Operations** (OP)—Includes suppliers/third parties, incident management, and backup and recovery operations
- **System access** (SA)—Includes both physical and information security

Subareas are optional and are grouped from particular control objectives—in this example (**figure E.1**), logical access and identity management.

Figure E.1—Example SOX ITGC Control Matrix

Control Area	Subarea	Appendix A Reference	COBIT 2019 Reference	Control Objective	Control Activity Test	I&T Risk Scenario Category	Level of Risk (High, Medium, Low)	Control Type (Automatic, Manual)	Control Category (Preventive, Detective, Corrective)	Summary of Findings	Documentation Cross-Reference (Number)
(SA) System Access	User Identity and Logical Access	Fig. A.10	DSS05.04 DSS06.03	Procedures exist and are followed to authenticate all users of the system (both internal and external) to support the existence of transactions.	Assess the authentication mechanisms used to validate user credentials for financial reporting systems and subsystems and validate that user sessions time out after a predetermined period of time. Validate that no shared user profiles (including administrative profiles) are used.	10	High				
(SA) System Access	User Identity and Logical Access	Fig. A.10	DSS05.01 DSS05.02 DSS05.03	Appropriate controls, including firewalls, intrusion detection and vulnerability assessments exist and are used to prevent unauthorized access via public networks.	Determine the sufficiency and appropriateness of perimeter security controls, including firewalls and intrusion detection systems (IDSs).	10	Medium				

Source: Adapted from ISACA, *IT Control Objectives for Sarbanes-Oxley: Using COBIT® 5 in the Design and Implementation of Internal Controls Over Financial Reporting, 3rd Edition*, USA, 2014, *https://store.isaca.org/s/store#/store/browse/detail/a2S4w000004Ko9JEAS*

Figure E.1—Example SOX ITGC Control Matrix *(cont.)*

Control Area	Subarea	Appendix A Reference	COBIT 2019 Reference	Control Objective	Control Activity Test	I&T Risk Scenario Category	Level of Risk (High, Medium, Low)	Control Type (Automatic, Manual)	Control Category (Preventive, Detective, Corrective)	Summary of Findings	Documentation Cross-Reference (Number)
(SA) System Access	User Identity and Logical Access	Fig. A.10	DSS05.01 DSS05.02 DSS05.03		Inquire whether management has performed an independent assessment of controls within the past year (e.g., ethical hacking, social engineering). Obtain a copy of this assessment and review the results, including the appropriateness of follow-up on identified weaknesses.	10	Medium				
(SA) System Access	User Identity and Logical Access	Fig. A.10	DSS05.01 DSS05.02 DSS05.03		Determine whether antivirus systems are used to protect the integrity and security of financial reporting systems and subsystems. When appropriate, determine whether encryption techniques are used to support the confidentiality of financial information sent from one system to another.	10	Medium				

Source: Adapted from ISACA, *IT Control Objectives for Sarbanes-Oxley: Using COBIT® 5 in the Design and Implementation of Internal Controls Over Financial Reporting, 3rd Edition*, USA, 2014, *https://store.isaca.org/s/store#/store/browse/detail/a2S4w000004Ko9JEAS*

Page intentionally left blank

APPENDIX F

Example Sarbanes-Oxley Control Narrative

The purpose of a SOX control narrative is to document the design and description of the internal control; a separate narrative is used to test the operating effectiveness.

This appendix provides an example SOC control narrative that analyzes one control application—systems access user identity and logical access (**figure F.1**); in reality, there will be many controls.

This example can be used as a template for control narratives.

Figure F.1—Example Sarbanes-Oxley Control Narrative Systems Access (SA): User Identity and Logical Access

		Control Type	Level of Risk
Control Objective	Procedures exist and are followed relating to timely action for requesting, establishing, issuing, suspending and closing user accounts. (Include procedures for authenticating transactions originating outside the enterprise, including contractors, vendors and third parties.) ★	KCA	H
COBIT 2019 reference	DSS05.04 Manage user identity and logical access.		
Process owner	Security administration group and help desk group		
Entity location	Washington DC		
Initial trigger (input)	Submission of new hire/change/separation form		
Starting point	Emails and designated forms are automatically imported into the help desk system.		
Completion point	Requested access is given or removed.		
Activity frequency	Daily		
Documentation	New hire setup form (separation form is secured)		
Success metrics	Number of user accounts (vs. number of authorized users/staff); number of incidents involving unauthorized user accounts		
Previous file reference	N/A		
Legend: Control Type: KCA = Key Control Area Level of Risk: L = Low, M = Medium, H = High			

Scope

The scope of the Systems Access: User Identity and Logical Access control narrative includes the following information:

- Descriptions of group responsibilities in this control narrative are only for those activities related to application access control.
- Descriptions are of in-scope applications, with the following exception:
    - The applications in this document do not include third-party SSAE 18 candidate applications.
- Two groups support the access control process:
    - A support center (SC) is responsible for maintaining standardized access forms and for technological support of help desk functionality, including automated notifications.

  - The security administration (sec admin) group is responsible for the bulk of access control provisioning activity for the in-scope applications and for defining the options on the standardized access forms.
- The ticketing system software is used to support the help desk. (Most enterprises use help desk software, of which there are numerous applications.)

Process Flow

Figure F.2 shows the Systems Access: User Identity and Logical Access process flow.

Figure F.2—Systems Access: User Identity and Logical Access Process Flow

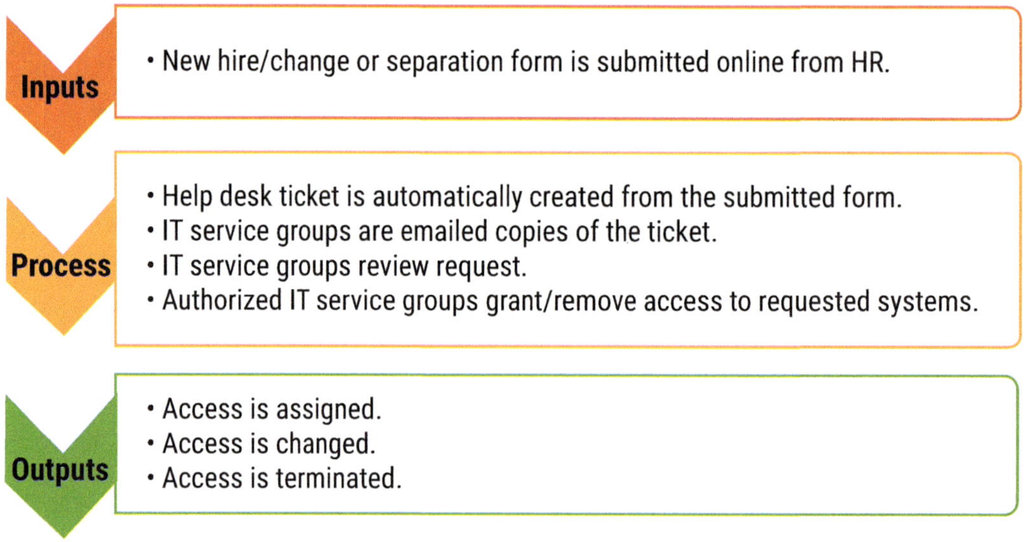

Source: Adapted from ISACA, *IT Control Objectives for Sarbanes-Oxley: Using COBIT® 5 in the Design and Implementation of Internal Controls Over Financial Reporting, 3rd Edition*, USA, 2014, *https://store.isaca.org/s/store#/store/browse/detail/a2S4w000004Ko9JEAS*

Process Narrative

The process narrative describes the Systems Access: User Identity and Logical Access detailed procedures and activities, including who performs the activities. **Figure F.3** shows the segregation of duties for the process.

Help Desk Access Security Process

New Hires/Changes

1. Managers fill out a standard new hire setup/change request form, which is available on the support center (SC) website for new hires. When the form is submitted, an email to the SC mailbox is automatically generated. In practice, the standard request form is not used for requests to change access levels of existing employees; managers send an email directly to the SC mailbox to request a change to access levels.
2. Emails to the SC website are imported into the help desk ticketing system. A work order ticket is automatically created and forwarded to the sec admin group mailbox and other defined service groups within the enterprise.

3. The sec admin group reviews the request and determines whether it requires action on the group's assigned applications/services. If action is required, access is granted or changed, and the ticket is marked completed. If action is not required, the ticket is marked completed. When all service groups have completed their copies of the ticket, the parent ticket is closed. A confirmation email is automatically sent to the requester.

Separations/Leaves/Terminations

1. Business managers call or email their local HR manager to request a separation form code, which is required to gain access to the separation form. The code is a validation code name for each day of the month. Each field and corporate HR manager keeps a copy of the code list. It is the responsibility of the HR manager to verify the legitimacy of the request.
2. At the SC website, business managers enter the code and access a standard separation form. When the form is electronically submitted, an email to the SC mailbox is automatically generated and imported into the help desk ticketing system. A work order ticket is automatically created and forwarded to the sec admin group mailbox and other defined service groups within the enterprise.
3. The sec admin group reviews the request and determines whether it requires action on the group's assigned applications/services. If action is required, access is terminated, and the ticket is marked completed. Access termination is inclusive of those supporting IT systems that are required to access the application (UNIX®, mainframe, databases). If action is not required, the ticket is marked completed. After all service groups have completed their copies of the ticket, the parent ticket is closed. A confirmation email is automatically sent to the requester.

Application-Specific Activity

SAP Application

The sec admin group performs all security administration activities for adding, deleting and changing access:

1. SAP® user ID and password are created/disabled (users are not deleted from the system).
2. Access levels are configured.
3. User ID is added to/deleted from the ERP Active Directory group to allow/remove access via Citrix® icon.

Process Deviation

The sec admin group contacts the requester via email to confirm whether the new user has been trained. Email confirmation verbiage is cut and pasted into the ticket.

Process Design Gap

Roles/jobs/profiles are defined for the SAP application, but not yet fully deployed to the new hire setup/change request form. Sec admin staff currently use the SAP application access role description spreadsheets to aid in the appropriate translation of the request. Requesting managers are using the current form. If additional information is required, sec admin staff communicates to the business for clarification.

Figure F.3—Segregation of Duties

Duties	Authorization	Security Administration Access	Recording	Verification
Add user.	• Manager-level employees • Defined approvers	• Security administration • Business personnel • IT personnel	Help desk ticket	Manager
Change user access.	• Manager-level employees • Defined approvers	• Security administration • Business personnel • IT personnel	Help desk ticket	Manager
Remove user access.	• HR	• Security administration • Business personnel • IT personnel	Help desk ticket	HR

APPENDIX G

Example Remediation Log

The purpose of a remediation log is to document and control all SOX remediation activities; outline the control gap, its associated risk and impact; and confirm the accountable control owner who has responsibility for mitigating the deficiency or material weakness. The example (**figure G.1**) in this appendix can be used as a template.

Figure G.1—Example Remediation Log

Number	Control Area	Control Ref.	Application Name or General IT Control Area	Control Design or Operating Effectiveness	Control Objective	Control Gap	Risk Status	Risk Description	Risk Impact	Recommendation	Control Owner	Classification (D = Deficiency, SD = Significant Deficiency, MW = Material Weakness)	Status (C = Communicated to Control Owner, I = In Process, R = Remediated)	Date Due	Comments
01	SD	App. A—Fig. A.4 BAI03.10	Managed Solutions Identification and Build	Control Design	The enterprise has a plan for the ongoing maintenance of the solutions developed and tested. This includes the periodic reviews against business needs and operational requirements.	Configuration requirements for the new SAP® application are not included in the control design plans, nor is capacity planning included in this process.	**High**	1. The systems cannot handle transaction volumes when user volumes increase. 2. The systems cannot handle the system load when new applications or initiatives are deployed.	**US$2M**	This is a critical area for the performance of SAP and needs to be urgently addressed. System sizing and capacity load planning should be immediately performed.	John Smith	SD	C	5 Apr 2022	
02	SA	App. A—Fig. A.10 DSS05.04 DSS06.03	User Identity and Logical Access	Operating Effectiveness	Procedures exist and are followed to authenticate all users of the system (both internal and external) to support the existence of transactions.	User access was not changed when users changed roles from one department to another, leading to incorrect access and log on to applications menus with shared access.	**High**	User time-out sessions and prompts for password changes were in operation, but some user profiles were shared, especially administrative profiles.	**US$1M**	This is a critical area in identity management. The sharing of administrative profiles can lead potentially to the risk of fraud.	Arthur B.	SD	C	10 Apr 2022	

Source: Adapted from ISACA, *IT Control Objectives for Sarbanes-Oxley: Using COBIT® 5 in the Design and Implementation of Internal Controls Over Financial Reporting, 3rd Edition*, USA, 2014, *https://store.isaca.org/s/store#/store/browse/detail/a2S4w000004Ko9JEAS*

Page intentionally left blank

APPENDIX H
Glossary

TERM	DEFINITION
American Institute of Certified Public Accountants (AICPA)	The national professional organization of certified public accountants in the United States, with more than 400,000 members. It sets ethical standards for the profession and US auditing standards for audits of private companies; nonprofit enterprises; federal, state and local governments.
Audit	Formal inspection and verification to check whether a standard or set of guidelines is being followed, records are accurate, or efficiency and effectiveness targets are being met *Scope Notes*: May be carried out by internal or external groups
Auditing Standard Board (ASB)	The senior committee of the AICPA, for auditing, attestation and quality control applicable to the performance and issuance of audit and attestation reports for private companies and nonprofit enterprises
Auditing Standard No. 2 (AS 2)	*An Audit of Internal Control Over Financial Reporting Performed in Conjunction With an Audit of Financial Statements*, developed by the Public Companies Accounting Oversight Board (PCAOB) and the first major SOX standard, published in 2003 (superseded by AS 5 on 15 November 2007)
Auditing Standard No. 5 (AS 5)	*An Audit of Internal Control Over Financial Reporting That Is Integrated With an Audit of Financial Statements*, which establishes requirements and provides directions that apply when an auditor conducts an audit on the system of ICFR See Audit
Auditor	An individual assigned to evaluate, audit or review an appraisal team leader or an appraisal
Automated application controls	Controls that have been programmed and embedded within an application
COSO	Committee of Sponsoring Organizations of the Treadway Commission *Scope Notes*: COSO's "Internal Control—Integrated Framework" is an internationally accepted standard for corporate governance. See *www.coso.org*.
Configurable control	Typically, an automated control that is based on and, therefore, dependent on the configuration of parameters within the application system
Control activities	The policies, procedures, techniques and mechanisms which help to ensure that management's response to reduce risk identified during the risk assessment process is carried out. For management of the effectiveness of internal control over financial reporting, control activities to test controls for SOX have been taken from the governance and management practice and activities in COBIT 5.
Control objective	A statement of the desired result or purpose to be achieved by implementing control procedures in a particular process

TERM	DEFINITION
Detective control	Designed to detect and report when errors, omissions and unauthorized uses or entries occur
Deficiency	A deficiency in internal control over financial reporting (ICFR) exists when the design or operation of a control does not allow management or employees, in the normal course of performing their assigned functions, to prevent or detect misstatements on a timely basis.
Entity-level controls	Internal controls which help to ensure that management directives pertaining to the entire entity are carried out. They are the second level of a top-down approach to understanding the risk of an enterprise. Generally, entity refers to the entire enterprise. Examples include: • Controls to monitor other controls, including activities of the internal audit function, the audit committee and self-assessment programs • Policies that address significant business control and risk management practices
Hybrid controls	Computer-dependent and consist of a combination of automated and manual controls
Internal control over financial reporting	A process designed by, or under the supervision of, the registrant's principal executive and principal financial officers, or persons performing similar functions, and effected by the registrant's board of directors, management and other personnel to provide reasonable assurance regarding the reliability of financial reporting and the preparation of financial statements for external purposes, in accordance with generally accepted accounting principals. Includes those policies and procedures that: • Pertain to the maintenance of records that in reasonable detail accurately and fairly reflect the transactions and dispositions of the assets of the registrant • Provide reasonable assurance that transactions are recorded as necessary to permit preparation of financial statements in accordance with generally accepted accounting principles, and that receipts and expenditures of the registrant are being made only in accordance with authorizations of management and directors of the registrant • Provide reasonable assurance regarding prevention or timely detection of unauthorized acquisition, use or disposition of the registrant's assets that could have a material effect on the financial statements
Internal controls	The policies, procedures, practices and organizational structures designed to provide reasonable assurance that business objectives will be achieved and undesired events will be prevented or detected and corrected
IT general controls	Described by the Public Companies Accounting Oversight Board (PCAOB) as controls embedded within IT processes that provide a reliable operating environment and support the effective operation of application controls

TERM	DEFINITION
Material weakness	A deficiency or a combination of deficiencies in internal control, such that there is a reasonable possibility that a material misstatement will not be prevented or detected on a timely basis.Weakness in control is considered 'material' if the absence of the control results in failure to provide reasonable assurance that the control objective will be met. A weakness classified as material implies that: • Controls are not in place and/or controls are not in use and/or controls are inadequate. • Escalation is warranted. There is an inverse relationship between materiality and the level of audit risk acceptable to the IS audit or assurance professional (i.e., the higher the materiality level, the lower the acceptability of the audit risk, and vice versa).
Public Companies Accounting Oversight Board (PCAOB)	A nonprofit corporation established by the US Congress to oversee the audits of public companies to protect the interests of investors and further the public interest in the preparation of informative, accurate and independent audit reports. PCAOB oversees the audits of broker-dealers, including compliance reports filed pursuant to federal securities laws, to promote investor protection.
Preventive control	An internal control that is used to avoid undesirable events, errors and other occurrences that an enterprise has determined could have a negative material effect on a process or end product
Sarbanes-Oxley Act of 2002 (SOX)	The US Sarbanes-Oxley Act of 2002 (PubL. 107-204, 116 Stat. 745, enacted 30 July 2002), also known as the "Public Company Accounting Reform and Investor Protection Act" (in the Senate) and "Corporate and Auditing Accountability and Responsibility Act" (in the House) and more commonly called Sarbanes-Oxley, Sarbox or SOX, is a US federal law that set new or enhanced standards for all US public company boards, management and public accounting firms.
Securities and Exchange Commission (SEC)	Agency of the US federal government. Holds primary responsibility for enforcing the federal securities laws and regulating the securities industry, the nation's stock and options exchanges, and other activities and enterprises, including the electronic securities markets in the United States.
Service Organization Control (SOC) Reports	Internal control reports on the services that are provided by a service organization and give valuable information that users need to assess and address the risk associated with an outsourced service
Software as a service (SaaS)	Offers the capability to use the provider's applications running on cloud infrastructure. The applications are accessible from various client devices through a thin client interface, such as a web browser (e.g., web-based email).
Statement on Standards for Attestation Engagements (SSAE) No. 18	SSAE 18, *Concepts Common to All Attestation Engagements*, was effective 1 May 2017 and replaced SSAE 16 and several other SSAEs. SSAE 18 is used to perform a variety of attestations, inclusive of service organization controls (SOC) attestations.

Page intentionally left blank

9781604208924